APR 2 4 2009

DATE DUE

D1297400

THE STUDENT LOAN SCAM

The Most Oppressive Debt
in U.S. History—and
How We Can Fight Back

ALAN COLLINGE

BEACON PRESS

BOSTON

Beacon Press
25 Beacon Street
Boston, Massachusetts 02108–2892
www.beacon.org

Beacon Press books
are published under the auspices of
the Unitarian Universalist Association of Congregations.

12 11 10 09   8 7 6 5 4 3 2 1

This book is printed on acid-free paper that meets the uncoated paper
ANSI/NISO specifications for permanence as revised in 1992.

Text design by Susan E. Kelly
at Wilsted & Taylor Publishing Services

Library of Congress Cataloging-in-Publication Data

Collinge, Alan
The student loan scam : the most oppressive debt in U.S. history—
and how we can fight back / Alan Collinge.
p. cm.
Includes bibliographical references and index.
ISBN-13: 978-0-8070-4229-8 (hardcover : alk. paper)
ISBN-10: 0-8070-4229-3 (hardcover : alk. paper)
1. Student loans—Corrupt practices—United States.
2. College graduates—United States—Finance, Personal.
3. Debt—United States. I. Title.

LB2340.2.C645 2008
378.3'620973—dc22   2008012230

Dedicated to my mother and father,
and to student loan borrowers everywhere

Contents

Preface

Being the poster child for defaulted student borrowers is a difficult job to have—and I never imagined I'd be known as the crusader for student loan justice. The truth is that I never considered student loans to be an especially interesting topic. College debt, I believed, was a necessary evil—to be repaid expeditiously and then forgotten even more quickly. However, what I once thought of as an uninteresting issue has come to dominate my life.

Over the course of earning three degrees in aerospace engineering at the University of Southern California, I managed to accumulate about thirty-eight thousand dollars in student loans. In 1998, when I graduated, these loans had grown to fifty thousand dollars, and I consolidated them with a friendly-sounding organization called Sallie Mae—an organization that at the time I believed was part of the federal government.

My plan was simple: graduate with a bulletproof education, get a fine job in my field, repay my loans, and let life blossom beyond that. I yearned for a simple, middle-class life—a wife, a family, and a house; typical cultural aspirations that I shared with most of the people in the blue-collar town in the Pacific Northwest where I grew up.

In late 1998, I found a job at an exceptionally good college, Caltech, as an aeronautical research scientist. The salary wasn't high, but, at thirty-five thousand dollars, it did just cover my rent; food; basic necessities, like a car and utilities; and my monthly student loan payment, which amounted to about 20 percent of my take-home pay.

In early 1999, I was slightly short on my student loan payment. I called the lender and was assured that as long as I continued to make my regularly scheduled payments, all would be well, with the exception of a one-time late fee on the account.

I continued to make regular payments; however, after around six months, I noticed that I had been charged a late fee every month since the initial underpayment. Assuming that this was a mistake, I called Sallie Mae and requested that the late fees be removed. To my surprise, they refused. I spoke to multiple Sallie Mae staff members, to no avail. It was then that I realized that Sallie Mae was not a government entity but, rather, a for-profit corporation. I searched for a different lender to take over my loans but found that these loans could not be refinanced—it was actually illegal to do so because of federal regulations that permit the consolidation of student loans one time only, whether or not there are other lenders willing to offer better terms on the loan.

It was becoming harder to keep up with my loan payments. My rent had increased, my utility costs had more than doubled, and a number of relatively small but significant unforeseen expenses had cropped up. By the summer of 2001, my financial situation had reached a critical state, and I decided to take radical steps to solve this problem. I resigned my position at Caltech, expecting to find a higher-paying position quickly, probably in the defense industry. Unfortunately, the events of September 11 put a chill on the economy, and instead of having a six-figure defense job, I was unemployed and surviving on a small retirement package. In retrospect, leaving Caltech without a job lined up was a big mistake, one that I will live with for the rest of my life.

I soon returned to my hometown of Tacoma, Washington. Nearly penniless, I slept on a friend's couch. I realized that my student loans were approaching default, and, on December 1, 2001, I applied for an economic-hardship forbearance. After all, I was unemployed; I should qualify. I didn't hear anything from Sallie Mae, and when I called a few days later, they claimed they had never received my application. I resubmitted the request. On December 13, Sallie Mae denied that request, and on December 14—the very next day—they put my loan in default. Nine days later, they made a payment claim for my loan for about sixty thousand dollars. I never received any notice from Sallie Mae explaining this. Calls to them garnered only the response "You'll have to call your guarantor. We no longer hold this loan."

I didn't realize then that it would be nearly two years before I found gainful employment. In the meantime, I took whatever kind of job I could find. I worked in five restaurants, and in 2002 I even spent four months cooking on a remote island in southeastern Alaska. I worked ninety-two hours a week, seven days a week, with no days off. My income, less than minimum wage, was not even close to covering the growth of my now-defaulted student loans. Sixteen months after Sallie Mae had defaulted my loans, a whopping eighteen thousand dollars had been added to my debt, far more than I had made during that time period. In the fall of 2002, when I returned from Alaska, I was shocked to find a bill from a collection company, General Revenue Corporation, for nearly eighty thousand dollars. The company, a subsidiary of Sallie Mae, was collecting on behalf of EdFund, the guarantor. I was baffled: Who were these two new companies, and what was a guarantor? I wasn't in a position to ask a wealthy relative for assistance, and the fact that the company was demanding "immediate payment in full" greatly increased my apprehension.

This began two years of relentless collection activities. I was inundated with calls from various collection companies, and at the same time, I was contacting my loan holders and attempting to negotiate a reasonable settlement. I tried Sallie Mae first, then EdFund and the various collection companies they used, and finally the U.S. Department of Education. I told them I'd repay the principal and accrued interest and even offered to pay at an increased interest rate of 10 percent if only they would remove some of the penalties. I believed that I was proposing a rather lucrative settlement; Sallie Mae had already made well over twenty-five thousand dollars on my original thirty-eight-thousand-dollar loan—why should they need more?

However, at every step along the way, I was refused. I found that I had no negotiation power whatsoever for my student loan debts: bankruptcy does not eliminate them, statutes of limitations do not exist for them, and the standard consumer protections on other types of debt do not apply. Meanwhile, my loan balance was exploding.

Most of the interactions, particularly with the collection companies, were unpleasant, to say the least. I was verbally assaulted, intimidated, and humiliated. I was called names that I have since suppressed in my memory. I was subjected to all manner of collection ploys designed to extract vast sums of money from me that I simply did not have.

It became apparent that I had been snared in a web of debt, the amount of which was now so far above what I had initially borrowed that it meant, in effect, a lifetime of indentured servitude. At this point I had a job at a nonprofit company and was making about three thousand dollars a month, but my debt had risen to nearly ninety-five thousand dollars. One day, at the age of thirty-three, I soberly recognized that my hopes for marriage, children, and a home were much farther away from being realized than they had been when I was twenty-nine, solely because of my mushrooming student loan debt.

I continued working obsessively. Between 2003 and 2005, I worked seven days a week, every week, with no days off, not even holidays. I earned a fixed salary, so this extra work was not for extra pay. In hindsight, I suspect I worked feverishly to somehow serve as a penance for my horrible student loan mistake. While this may have had cathartic benefits, it did nothing to reduce my debt; by mid-2005, my balance had swollen to $103,000.

Those who have had similar experiences will understand when I say that the debt overwhelmed and paralyzed me. It was completely demoralizing. All the extreme effort, personal sacrifice, late nights studying, and poverty-level subsistence had been endured for the sake of higher education; because of the loans, that education had ended up doing me far more harm than good. I felt like the butt of a very expensive, lifelong joke.

In the spring of 2004, something snapped. I became obsessed, literally unable to put my student loans out of my mind for more than a couple of hours at a time. I was furious at myself, frustrated at the sheer stupidity of the situation—and just plain angry.

Consumed, I began doing research. I found that Sallie Mae and other lenders made far more money from defaulted loans than they did from those that remained in good standing. Sallie Mae's stock price had actually shot up significantly in the aftermath of the dot-com collapse, and between 1995 and 2005, it had risen by 1,700 percent—the company was truly a Wall Street darling. I found that executives at both Sallie Mae and EdFund had amassed personal fortunes in the period of time since I had graduated—in one instance, enough for an executive to attempt to purchase a Major League Baseball team. I found that well-connected student loan executives and shareholders had carefully orchestrated a lobbying campaign to strip away even the most basic consumer protections from student loans. I found that even the federal government was making—not losing—massive amounts of money from the business of defaulted loans, and I found that the Department of Education's Office of Federal Student Aid was being run by former student loan company executives. Finally—and perhaps most important—I found that I wasn't alone: millions of other citizens were trapped just as I was.

This is a crisis that our country has never before had to face. In a very real sense, it threatens to subjugate large segments of our population, trapping citizens into lifetimes of debt at the cost of pursuits that could be far more beneficial to the nation's interests.

I decided I basically had three options. The first was to accept my fate and live at the poverty level while I paid off this exploded debt, which would probably take me well into my fifties or sixties to do. The second option, I'm embarrassed to admit, was to escape the debt entirely, either by fleeing the country or by remaining here and assuming a new identity. The last option was to try and force a political solution by connecting with the millions of people who shared my fate, exposing the individuals who had engineered—and profited tremendously from—this uniquely predatory system, and helping to spur Congress to fix the problem.

Option number one was probably the easiest choice and, incidentally, the one that the vast majority of student loan debtors take. However, I decided to embrace the last option. I realized it would require dedication, years of effort, and (probably) a great deal of luck to accomplish, and that I might very well compromise any future career, reputation, and earning potential in the field for which I had gone to school.

In March 2005 I started a Web site called StudentLoanJustice.org; I posted my research there and invited others to share their stories. The purpose of SLJ was (and is) to convince Congress to restore standard consumer protections to student loans. This would allow millions of borrowers to negotiate fair and reasonable settlements of their student loans, just as borrowers do for their credit cards, payday loans, and IRS debt.

Since I was virtually invisible on the Internet and had no budget, marketing or otherwise, I had humble expectations. However, to my amazement, by the end of the year hundreds of people had posted their stories on the Web site. I received submissions from people whose debts had exploded far more astoundingly than my own; for instance, there was one couple who had already paid more than double their original loan amounts but who still owed more than double what they had borrowed. There were people who had left the country, even people whose family members had committed suicide as a result of overwhelming student loan debt. Despite the sometimes tragic circumstances that united us, we were comforted by the connection to others who had experienced similar realities.

I made multiple mistakes in the organization's first year, many of which were emotionally driven. Calling the Sallie Mae CEO at three in the morning, for instance, was not a wise decision, nor was sending an e-mail containing expletives to a lobbyist whom I found particularly offensive. These were early blunders, but my research was solid, and the facts that I compiled, combined with stories from real citizens, painted a compelling picture.

I'm grateful that several useful accomplishments emerged that year. I implored Bethany McLean, the well-known financial journalist who broke the Enron story, to examine the issue; after over a year of communication with me, she wrote an exceptionally strong article that was published in December 2005 in *Fortune* magazine. StudentLoanJustice.org was featured in the article, something that amazed me. Sallie Mae responded with a lengthy and scathing criticism of both the piece and my repayment history. The *Baltimore Sun* published an op-ed I wrote on the subject, and shortly thereafter, in March 2006, I and three other StudentLoanJustice.org members were in the New York City Women's Republican Club being interviewed by Lesley Stahl of *60 Minutes*.

The *60 Minutes* segment ended up being the top story of that week's edition, and it ran on May 7, 2006. This was progress almost beyond what I had hoped for. When both Ralph Nader and Michael Moore contacted the organization the week following the show, it became apparent that we had touched a nerve with the American public. The avalanche of press coverage has included such publications as the *Washington Post,* the *New York Times,* the *Los Angeles Times,* the *Chicago Sun-Times,* the *San Francisco Chronicle,* and the *Chronicle of Higher Education,* among many others. Members of the organization have been guests on numerous radio programs, including NPR, and the organization has been featured on Fox TV and in local investigative reports.

The news media has proven to be absolutely critical to the success of this movement. Indeed, around the time the *60 Minutes* piece aired, Senator Hillary Clinton's office worked with us to craft the Student Borrower Bill of Rights. If this important legislation had been passed, it would have done much to restore basic consumer protections to student loans; we were credited as being the reason her office had decided to pursue the issue.

In December 2006, I was laid off from a low-level defense job after I'd failed to obtain a security clearance. (During the security-clearance interview, the issue of student loans was the first, and nearly only, topic discussed.) Given this development, I decided to form a political action committee, and I toured the country in a beat-up RV, meeting with staffers from both the House and Senate Education Committees and giving talks at local universities and other gatherings.

The past three years have been a whirlwind of activity. Some significant progress has been made, but I occasionally wonder how my life would have unfolded without the specter of student loans. I'd never have imagined that I'd be devoting so much unpaid effort to any cause, and yet I have the conviction that I'm doing the right thing for the public good. At this point, I think it's important to write this book so that others facing similar situations can be informed and also help move the public debate on this issue toward a workable solution.

In this book, I will examine the history of the student loan industry and analyze its current state. You will read about the industry's dizzying corporate profits, about the organizations and individuals it benefits, and, most important, about the many people whose lives it has destroyed. Student loans have become the most profitable (for the industry) and oppressive (for the borrowers) type of debt in our nation's history, mostly as a result of federal legislation since the mid-1990s that has removed standard consumer protections and provided the lending industry with draconian collection tools to use against the borrowers. This book will not only shine a bright light on this problem but suggest concrete and pragmatic solutions for the future.

CHAPTER ONE

The Rise of Sallie Mae and the Fall of Consumer Protections

Student loans barely existed forty years ago. Today, however, U.S. citizens borrow close to ninety billion dollars a year in order to attend college, and this amount is growing at an alarming rate. An industry that was virtually nonexistent in decades past has grown to dominate the lives of millions of educated Americans. And at the same time as student debt grew, most standard consumer protections were removed from this type of debt, with the result that today, student loans have a stranglehold on millions of lower- and middle-class citizens.

After World War II, the United States took extraordinary measures to enable citizens to achieve the American dream. This included building a nation where people of all income levels could afford to attend college. Prior to the war, college educations were largely the province of the well-to-do, completely out of reach for low- and middle-income Americans, the vast majority of whom did not even finish high school. When President Roosevelt signed the GI Bill in 1944, this began to change.

As the nation beat its swords into plowshares, Roosevelt recognized that it was critical to give returning soldiers opportunities to rejoin the American culture; they had to be offered real chances for prosperity. Hard lessons had been learned from World War I, after which returning military personnel each got sixty dollars and a train ticket, and nothing more. These veterans found it difficult to earn a living upon their return, and during the Depression, they even organized a protest in Washington, D.C., seeking payment of long-overdue service bonuses. This twenty-thousand-man-strong Bonus Army set up encampments near the White House, and many refused to leave even when they were ordered to. Violence ensued, and two veterans were killed. This marked one of the greatest periods of unrest the capital had known[1] and was certainly one of the factors that was considered when the GI Bill was created.

In addition to providing loan guarantees for housing and assistance for unemployed veterans, the GI Bill covered college tuition for servicemen and servicewomen up to five hundred dollars per year and also paid them a monthly living allowance while they pursued their studies. Of the three elements of the GI Bill, free access to higher education was by far the most widely used. By 1947, nearly 50 percent of all new college students were returning military personnel, and by the time the original GI Bill expired, in 1956, a remarkable 7.6 million Americans had utilized the program.[2]

By the 1960s, the global political landscape had changed. Communism was perceived as an urgent threat to democracy in America and throughout the world. The Cold War was in full swing, and the Space Race had begun. There was a critical demand for engineers and scientists to support these efforts, and America's colleges and universities were needed more than ever to equip citizens for these positions; the federal government—primarily the Department of Defense—invested heavily in them for this purpose.

Despite the success of the GI Bill, the nation remained largely uneducated: only one person in four possessed a high school diploma, and a far smaller percentage of the population had college degrees. In addition, poverty was still a widespread problem in the country. President Lyndon Johnson, who had taught at an impoverished south Texas school before the war, recognized that higher education was crucial not only to the nation's security and defense but also to its economic and social development. In his 1963 Education Message, Johnson noted, "Poverty has many roots, but the taproot is ignorance."[3]

A key element of Johnson's Great Society was embodied in the Higher Education Act of 1965. This landmark piece of legislation provided a wide array of funding for college students, including grant and scholarship programs. The Higher Education Act also provided loan guaranties to banks in order to promote the banks' lending to students who wished to pursue postsecondary education.

By the end of the decade, the nation had made formidable strides to meet its goals of providing low- or no-cost college education to the public. From 1960 to 1970, the nation's population increased by about 16 percent, but the number of adults holding four-year degrees increased by about 67 percent. For non-white Americans, this number increased far more dramatically, by over 200 percent.[4] Also, when students realized that they could afford to go to college, high school graduation rates surged, from roughly 63 percent to almost 80 percent.[5] Owing to investment in both teaching development and brick-and-mortar projects, the capacity of universities, community colleges, and trade schools nationwide increased similarly. In addition, the median number of years in school for the country's citizens went from 10.6 to 12.1 years.[6]

The benefits to the nation were everywhere. National security improved significantly (although the Cold War would continue for another two decades). By 1969, the United States had landed men on the moon and brought them home safely, as promised by President Kennedy. The accompanying spin-off technologies in nearly all engineering disciplines are too numerous to mention. The computing revolution had taken root at university research centers across the country, and in the early

1970s, ARPAnet—later to become the Internet—was developed and deployed at the nation's universities. Because of these substantial achievements, the U.S. higher education system became the envy of the world—a gratifying return on the investment.

In 1970, the average amount of a university's tuition and fees was about $585 per student per year,[7] and only a small minority of students required loans to attend. The few students who did require loans were typically able to repay them—at least anecdotally—in months, not years. From the citizen's perspective, these were the best of times for higher education. Sadly, these glory days were numbered, and citizens growing up in subsequent decades faced a starkly different reality.

The New Reality

The halcyon days of higher education in the early 1970s, when the typical high school graduate could put him- or herself through college for a few thousand dollars (at most) in student loan debt and be able to repay this debt by working over the summers, are long gone. Today, about two-thirds of college students require loans to make it through, and the typical undergraduate borrower leaves school with more than twenty thousand dollars in student loan debt. For graduate students, that amount more than doubles, to forty-two thousand dollars. Tuition inflation has outpaced the consumer price index (CPI) during this time period by a factor of about two to one.

Also during this period, the Higher Education Act was amended six times, becoming progressively more lucrative for the lenders and less beneficial for the students. Over time, legislators gave more support to the interests of the student loan companies and the federal government than to the interests of the students. Bankruptcy protections, statutes of limitations, refinancing rights, and many other standard consumer protections vanished for student loans—and only for student loans. Concurrently, draconian collection tools were legislated into existence, and they provided unprecedented and unrivaled collection powers to the loan industry, including giving it the ability to garnishee a borrower's wages, tax returns, Social Security, and disability income—all without a court order. Today, the student loan is an inescapable and profitable debt instrument unlike any other.

This lack of consumer protections has proven to be extremely beneficial for student loan companies, which were already guaranteed repayment of nearly the full unpaid balance of the loans in case of default. Student loan companies now realize extreme profits, not only because they collect interest on the loans from borrowers and special allowance (subsidy) payments from the federal government, but also because they collect penalties and fees on defaulted debt from the students who encountered financial difficulties repaying the original loans. Defaulted student loan debt with penalties, fees, collection charges, and compounded interest can double or triple the original balance—or worse. Ralph Nader wrote in 2006 that "the corporate lawyers who conceived this self-enriching system ought to get the nation's top prize for shameless perversity."[8]

Albert Lord, chief executive officer of Sallie Mae, the most dominant student loan company in the United States, reported to shareholders in 2003 that the company's record profits were attributable to penalties and fees collected from defaulted loans. Indeed, Sallie Mae's fee income increased by 228 percent (from $280 million to $920 million) between 2000 and 2005,[9] while its managed loan portfolio increased by only 82 percent (from $67 billion to $122 billion) during the same time period.[10] Prior to the sub-prime mortgage credit crisis of 2007 to 2008, the company's stock had shot up by more than 1,600 percent between 1995 and 2005—an average annual rise of about 160 percent.

The company transformed from a government-sponsored entity to a for-profit corporation in 1995, and it set aside $3.6 billion in stock for its employees—equivalent to $639,000 per employee.[11] As of April 2007, the top two executives at Sallie Mae, Albert Lord and Tim Fitzpatrick, have together made more than half a billion dollars. Lord even attempted to purchase a Major League Baseball team, the Washington Nationals, in 2005.[12]

The penalties and collection costs associated with defaulted student loans have proven to be lucrative for the federal government as well. Surprisingly, for every dollar the U.S. Department of Education pays to lenders for defaulted loans, the department gets back every dollar of principal, plus about 20 percent in interest and fees.[13] On the face of it, it seems absurd that any entity, private or government, can actually find a way to make—not lose—money from borrowers who default on their debts, but this is indeed the new reality.

As many borrowers can attest, the student loan system in general can be overwhelmingly confusing. Most students receive multiple types of loans from several different lenders, and these loan amounts are determined by opaque processes within their universities' financial aid departments and by the federal government. Most students cannot identify their lenders, and some are confused about how much they have borrowed. In the rush to get registered for classes, only a tiny fraction of students read and understand the terms of their loans.

This confusion and lack of knowledge play directly into the hands of the student loan companies. They often have so-called preferred-lender arrangements with the universities, which means that the school steers students toward a small number of lenders in exchange for financial rewards from those lenders. Thus, the schools make additional money—what amounts to a kickback—over and above tuition charges.

Borrower Horror Stories

Predictably, this system has taken an extreme toll on the unfortunate borrowers caught in the trap. A typical example of this phenomenon can be seen from the case of Britt Napoli, a college counselor in northern California. In the late 1980s and early 1990s, he borrowed about thirty thousand dollars to attend graduate school at Cal State, Northridge. In 1993, after an earthquake destroyed his apartment near campus, Britt's loans were placed in default status without his knowledge.

The default of Napoli's loans began a process that he describes as a "student loan hell." His loans quickly began to grow with penalties, fees, and collection costs. Britt tried to negotiate a reasonable payment plan for these loans but was denied at every step. By 2008, through wage and tax-refund garnishments, Napoli had repaid about thirty-three thousand dollars but still owed about seventy thousand. Now approaching his fiftieth birthday, Napoli wonders how secure his Social Security benefits are, given that this income is garnishable by the federal government for the repayment of defaulted student loans. "It's unbelievable that I've still got so much to repay—there's no end to this nightmare in sight," Napoli says, sighing.

Believing that his student loans would be forgiven if he taught in an underserved community—something that is advertised frequently to student borrowers—Napoli worked for five years as a counselor at an elementary school in south-central Los Angeles. In the last year of his term, Napoli attempted to pursue forgiveness of the loan, only to find out that defaulted loans did not qualify for forgiveness. He says that he was naïve to believe that his loans would be forgiven and regrets not having more fully explored this option prior to his work in Los Angeles.

In the meantime, his wages had been garnished, his tax refunds seized. Napoli states with frustration, "I've lived like a second-class citizen—like a felon—all these years, allowing my paychecks to be dunned and my taxes to be taken." He pauses, then says, "I've attempted to deal with what I thought were government agencies that held my loans, only to be rebuffed by them because they like things exactly the way they are. They don't need to negotiate, and so they don't. It's as simple as that."

The effect of these loans on Napoli's life has been significant. He had intended to pursue a PhD in psychology at the University of Southern California, but he couldn't. He found that he did not qualify for financial aid because he had defaulted loans on his record. When choosing his current job, he decided to work near Sacramento partly so that he could deal in person with his loan holder, EdFund, a nonprofit guaranty agency. Napoli visited EdFund headquarters to meet personally with a representative to discuss his loans, but he was escorted out of the facility by security. Napoli describes EdFund headquarters as "like an expensive fortress, with multiple layers of security, including guards and cameras—the whole nine yards. With over a decade of paying on this, and with the benefit of hindsight, I have to wonder if they wanted borrowers to default on their loans all along. Otherwise, they wouldn't exist. Building Ed-Fund's castle is where my money went."

Analysis of EdFund's IRS form 990 filings reveal that their class-A facility in Rancho Cordova, California, is not the only place that Napoli's money is going. The executives and attorneys working at EdFund have realized explosive growth in their salaries since 1997. This is detailed in the next chapter and also in the appendix.

Currently, Napoli is pondering quitting his job and relocating with his wife out of the country in order to regain financial control over his life. "This debt has permeated every aspect of my life. I don't sleep well at night. I worry constantly about what assets I do have." Napoli continues, "It depresses me to think what my life could have been like without this debt hanging over my head, sucking every spare nickel out of me. As I get older and this student loan debt continues to spiral, I think more and more often that this is not a country I want to live in." Of course, leaving the country is not a palatable option for Britt, particularly having to do it for the sole purpose of escaping his enormous student loan burden.

The Rise of Sallie Mae

It is impossible to discuss the explosive growth of the student loan industry without examining the evolution of Sallie Mae from a government-sponsored entity to the dominant for-profit corporation in the business. Given the company's control of the student loan industry from the start and its gorilla-like strength on Capitol Hill, the story of the growth of the student loan industry really is a story about the growth of Sallie Mae.

In 1972, President Richard Nixon signed legislation that established the Student Loan Marketing Association (Sallie Mae). Sallie Mae was formed for the purpose of encouraging banks, schools, and other lenders to make loans to college students; Sallie Mae would then purchase these loans, thus serving as a secondary market for them.

Initially, Sallie Mae was a government-sponsored entity (GSE) and was completely dependent on the U.S. Treasury for its operations. Much of the funding used by Sallie Mae to purchase loans and provide services to students was provided by the U.S. Treasury, and the Treasury had charge of its oversight. However, the company was allowed to take on investors by design, and two-thirds of the board of directors was elected by shareholders. The company is often compared to other GSEs, such as Fannie Mae, which performs a similar function in the home mortgage industry.

The creation of Sallie Mae signaled the continuation and expansion of a trend that had begun with the passage of the Higher Education Act of 1965: namely, shifting the financial burden of attending college from the government to the students. This trend was described in a 1974 groundbreaking article by Larry L. Leslie and Gary P. Johnson of Penn State University[14] in which they noted that traditional federal and state funding of universities was decreasing while funding in the form of loans and grant aid to students was increasing. In effect, the government was acting to realize the public benefit of higher education without making the corresponding investment in it.[15] According to Dr. Leslie, this shift away from traditional funding of institutions of higher learning and toward student aid was "doomed from the beginning" and is a primary cause for the spiraling cost of college that we see today. Dr. Leslie also feels that this policy has "greatly damaged the support of the middle class, who now pay their high taxes, then must turn around and pay high costs for their children."[16]

Albert Lord, a Penn State graduate, joined the executive staff of Sallie Mae in 1981. Around this time, Sallie Mae began to use its influence with Congress to expand its operations, and it grew significantly in both volume and scope. Sallie Mae began to consolidate loans, for instance, and was realizing significant returns on the loans that it had purchased. By 1991, Sallie Mae owned about a third of the forty-nine-billion-dollar market of outstanding federally guaranteed student loans. Also in 1991, Lord became Sallie Mae's chief operating officer.

In 1993, in response to growing criticism by policy makers that banks were growing rich through excessive subsidies provided by the federal government for student loans, President Clinton signed legislation that created the Federal Direct Loan Program. The concept of the Direct Loan Program was to bypass the middlemen and loan money to college students directly, thereby saving taxpayers significant monies that would have otherwise gone to the banks. Some Sallie Mae executives and shareholders, most notably Albert Lord, viewed this as a direct threat to the Sallie Mae organization. In the first two years of operation of the Direct Loan Program, Sallie Mae lost about half of its market value,[17] and Direct Loans grew to about 34 percent of the student loan market. Lord believed that the company should be more aggressive and expand its operations to capitalize more fully on the growing student loan market—and take back what the Direct Loan Program had gained. Lord and other shareholders formed a coalition dubbed the Committee to Restore

Value, and a lengthy proxy battle ensued. In 1995, Lord was successful in capturing control of Sallie Mae's board of directors, and he was appointed CEO.

In 1997, Lord assumed control of privatizing Sallie Mae, and he decided to meet the federal loan problem head-on. This was accomplished in several ways. First, Sallie Mae greatly expanded its operations and began making loans directly to students. The company was in an excellent position to do this: it had universal brand recognition, and the Sallie Mae name carried the faith and credit of the federal government in the eyes of university financial aid offices and the public.

Sallie Mae exploited practices that the administrators and staff of the Direct Loan Program couldn't. For instance, the company began signing up schools in school-as-lender programs, whereby the universities actually made money on their students' loans if those loans went through Sallie Mae. To secure universities' commitments to putting Sallie Mae on their preferred-lender lists, the company offered various perks to financial aid officials, including all-expenses-paid trips to exotic locations, golf outings, lavish parties, and the like.[18] In the words of Ellen Frishberg, the financial aid director for Johns Hopkins University, who was recently forced to resign after she accepted stock and other benefits from a student loan company, "It's an endless stream of invitations; it's quite comical at times."[19]

Sallie Mae also used their allies on Capitol Hill to undermine the federal program. Sallie Mae and a handful of other student loan interests spent millions of dollars lobbying Congress in the mid-1990s. Key legislators' campaign committees and PACs were funded through this effort, and "fact-finding missions" to places such as Boca Raton were sponsored by the company and attended by these legislators and their staff. Some legislators' family members even benefited from these cozy relationships. Most notably, during a game of golf with a student loan company executive, John Boehner, then chairman of the House Committee on Education and the Workforce, secured a job for his daughter at a student loan collection company, General Revenue Corporation.[20] This company was acquired shortly thereafter by Sallie Mae.

The lobbying paid off. Throughout the 1990s and into the beginning of the twenty-first century, the Republican Congress made repeated attempts to starve the Direct Loan Program by putting its funding into an account held at the discretion of Congress—making the program easier to kill. Congress also passed laws that made Sallie Mae's loans more profitable through enhanced subsidies, thus allowing them to be more competitive against the Direct Loans, although at a high cost to the taxpayer. Despite the fact that multiple studies confirmed that the Direct Loan Program was significantly cheaper for the federal government than other options, the Bush administration perpetuated "a slow strangulation of the student loan program," according to Barmak Nassirian, a highly regarded industry expert.[21] By 2006, the share of the Federal Direct Loan Program had diminished to about 19 percent of the market.[22]

Sallie Mae Marches Toward Monopoly

Sallie Mae was not satisfied with being merely a student lender. The company wanted control of all aspects of the student loan industry: loans, guaranties, and collections. Thus began a monopolistic, acquisitional crusade by Sallie Mae. In 1999, Sallie Mae purchased Nellie Mae, a nonprofit student loan company based in Braintree, Massachusetts. This was followed quickly by the purchase of two of the nation's largest nonprofit student loan guarantors, the USA Group, in Indianapolis, and Southwest Student Services. In a one-week period in 2002, Sallie Mae purchased two of the largest student loan collection companies, Pioneer Credit Recovery (Arcade, New York) and General Revenue Corporation (Cincinnati). In 2004, Sallie Mae acquired another collection company, Arrow Financial Services (based in Niles, Illinois), and in August 2005, yet another, GRP Financial Services (based in White Plains, New York).

By 2006, Sallie Mae virtually dominated the student loan industry. It was about four times larger than its nearest competitor (Citibank), managed $123 billion in student loans, and by Wall Street's standards had become a stock-market rock star. It was now the largest player in all three parts of the student loan industry: loans, guaranties, and collections.

Notably, Sallie Mae had also become the nation's largest provider of *private* student loans. Such private loans, which are not guaranteed by the federal government, now account for 20 percent of all student loans and are extremely profitable for the lenders; although there are no federal subsidies for the loans, they typically carry with them interest rates far exceeding those of federally guaranteed loans. Interest rates of 18 percent or higher are not uncommon in the industry, and the national average interest rate is approximately 12 percent. Sallie Mae has been found to charge APRs of as high as 28 percent.[23]

Thus far, Sallie Mae's rise may appear to be a typical success story in American enterprise. After all, those companies that provide better products or services to their customers should succeed and thrive. But as this book will show, Sallie Mae was *not* a better company providing a better product or service to its customers. Rather, it was a politically sophisticated corporation that lobbied its way to extreme profitability at the expense of students and taxpayers. It used an unfair advantage bestowed on it by Congress to take over the industry and extract vast sums of unearned capital from misfortunate borrowers.

The Fall of Consumer Protections

In the 1990s, the new, privatized Sallie Mae gained control over the industry, and it used its power on Capitol Hill to great effect, convincing Congress to strip away nearly all consumer protections from student loans. It also lobbied for—and got—legislation that allowed for massive penalties and fees for delinquent debt, legislation that actually made it more profitable for the lenders and guarantors when students defaulted than when they paid. Senator Ted Kennedy, who was minority leader of the Senate Education Committee until 2007, when he became majority leader, remarked before an Education Committee meeting in the spring of that year, "At every reauthorization, we kept sweetening the deal for banks, sweetening the pot." He lamented the fact that this deal sweetening progressed until it reached the point where companies profited more from students defaulting than from students keeping their loans in good standing.[24]

By 2006, student loans had fewer consumer protections than any other type of loan instrument in the nation's history. In 1976, Congress had passed a law making federally guaranteed student loans nondischargeable in bankruptcy; this meant that declaring bankruptcy did not erase the loan. Initially, a provision in the law stated that this only held true for five years, after which the loans could be discharged in bankruptcy. A further provision permitted the loans to be dischargeable if the debtor could prove undue hardship.[25] In 1990, Congress extended the five years to seven, but watershed legislation that was part of the 1998 Higher Education Act reauthorization abolished this provision altogether. At that time, and still today, student loans are the only type of loan in U.S. history to be nondischargeable in bankruptcy. According to one borrower who found herself in bankruptcy court, "The judge told me not to come back unless I was in a wheelchair."

One might suspect that the student loan industry would be satisfied with the removal of this basic, standard consumer protection for federally guaranteed loans, but it still wasn't content. In 2005, the Bankruptcy Abuse Prevention and Consumer Protection Act was passed. Stealthily inserted into this bill was language that in effect made *all* student loans, even those that were *not* guaranteed by the federal government, nondischargeable in bankruptcy. This language was never debated by Congress, and the bill became law on October 17, 2005. The legislation was seen by experts as incontrovertible proof that the student loan industry, more than any other lending industry, held sway over the U.S. Congress.[26]

In addition to removing bankruptcy protections, the amendments to the Higher Education Act eliminated all statutes of limitations for the collection of student loan debt. This opened up a whole new market: old loans from the 1970s and 1980s suddenly became collectible debt. Student loans were also specifically exempted from state usury laws, and they were even exempted from coverage under the Truth in Lending Act (TILA). In 1988, the Federal Trade Commission issued a determination that nonprofit, state-run student loan agencies did not have to adhere to the Fair Debt Collection and Practices Act. This meant that most student loan guarantors could ignore this legislation when pursuing defaulted borrowers.[27]

From the beginning of the federally guaranteed student loan program, there were no obvious mechanisms for refinancing student loans after graduation and for consolidation of the loans. In other words, once a student graduated and consolidated his or her loans, he or she could never leave that lender, even if there were other lenders who were willing to offer better terms. The freedom to change lenders in order to find better terms for a loan is a consumer protection that is taken for granted in every other lending industry, but it is nonexistent for student loans. In fact, legislation was passed that required a borrower to consolidate his loans with the original lender (if there was only one original lender). In effect, the student loan companies had an iron grip on the borrower for the life of the loans. However, an enterprising student loan executive at a small student loan company found a loophole in the federal law whereby a borrower could transfer his or her loans through the Direct Loan Program and into the Federal Family Education Loan (FFEL) Program with a different lender.

This procedure, dubbed the Super Two-Step within the industry, was complicated and cumbersome. Nonetheless, borrowers were so dissatisfied with the large lenders that they clamored to take advantage of this means of refinancing their debt. Predictably, Sallie Mae and the other big lenders, such as Citibank, moved swiftly to close this loophole. It certainly didn't hurt that the head of the House Education Committee, John Boehner, received the largest amount of Sallie Mae's PAC money and that his daughter, Tricia, worked for General Revenue Corporation, a subsidiary of Sallie Mae. Similarly, on the Senate side, the Education Committee's majority leader, Mike Enzi, ran a PAC that was largely funded by student loan interests. In 2005, the refinancing loophole was closed. Sallie Mae spokesperson Tom Joyce confidently predicted that with the closing of the Super Two-Step, smaller lenders would "think twice" about entering the student loan market.

Despite landmark legislation passed by a Democrat-controlled Congress in September 2007, touted as the most significant bill for students since the GI Bill, the lack of standard consumer protections for student borrowers remained. Legislative proposals to restore consumer protections, such as Senator Hillary Clinton's Student Borrower Bill of Rights, were introduced, but they somehow never made it into the 2007 legislation. On this point, the student loan industry again had its way with Congress. All the protections that had been removed to protect the interests of the banks and the government remained unavailable to the overwhelming majority of student loan borrowers.

Collection Powers

In addition to removing standard consumer protections, Congress passed legislation that made delinquent student loan debt highly lucrative for the student loan industry. This legislation allowed massive penalties and fees, and Congress permitted the industry to use draconian collection methods to recover this increased debt. Most of these congressional giveaways to the industry were included in the 1998 amendments to the Higher Education Act and were pushed fiercely by the student loan industry. "In American history, this is the most outrageous giveaway ever extended by the federal government to private lenders," says Barmak Nassirian, associate executive director of the American Association of Collegiate Registrars and Admissions Officers.

This legislation provided for collection rates of up to 25 percent to be applied to the debt. This meant that when borrowers defaulted on their loans, guarantors could take a quarter of every dollar the borrowers eventually repaid, money that would not be applied to the principal and interest on the debts, which the borrowers had been unable to afford to repay in the first place. This massive, unearned revenue stream going to the guarantors and to the collection agencies they contract with (agencies that are often owned by the original lenders) has not surprisingly led to usurious situations. These prompted a Senate investigation in 2007, described in chapter 3. A few of the specific cases investigated, such as that of Britt Napoli, are described elsewhere in this book.

Congress provided the loan guarantors and collection companies with "powers that would make a mobster envious," according to Harvard professor Elizabeth Warren. These powers included wage, Social Security, and disability garnishment, as well as tax seizure, suspension of state-issued professional licenses, and even termination of public employment.

The legislation has proven to be extremely lucrative and profitable for Sallie Mae. Indeed, in the 2003 Sallie Mae annual report, Albert Lord bragged to shareholders that their record profits that year were attributable in part to fees and penalties collected on defaulted loans.[28] Lord's successor, Tim Fitzpatrick, has made similar claims in subsequent years in reports to share-holders.[29]

Making defaulted student loans expensive for the borrower but lucrative and easy to collect on for the collection agencies has given rise to companies such as Premiere Credit of North America, an Indianapolis collection company specializing in student loans. Premiere has done an amazing business in the past decade; they have even seen fit to install a four-thousand-gallon shark tank in the lobby of their corporate headquarters to inspire their workers.

Who We Are

There are more than five million defaulted loans on record with the U.S. Department of Education, totaling nearly forty billion dollars. There are millions more borrowers who have "paid their way" out, somehow coming up with the money for penalties and fees so that their loans could be removed from default status. For every defaulted borrower, there is probably another borrower who remains just barely out of default. There are also many defaulted private student loans—that is, loans that are not guaranteed by the federal government but which are nonetheless not dischargeable in bankruptcy. Given that private loans made up about a fifth of the industry in 2007, it is reasonable to estimate that there are perhaps one million private loans in default status and an equal number of private loans perilously close to defaulting.

Those individuals who are negatively affected by the student loan system are as diverse as the American population. They include members of a wide range of professions, from blue-collar to white-collar, but they all share a reluctance to speak publicly about their situations. The embarrassment, humiliation, and intimidation that borrowers feel when their loans spiral out of control or when they are trapped in predatory lending situations prevent most from speaking out. Some are even too embarrassed to tell their families about their defaulted loans.

There is David, a chiropractor in Texas, who originally borrowed seventy thousand dollars for college. After David was unemployed for a period during the mid-1990s, his loans defaulted, and to date they have escalated to about four hundred thousand dollars. The State of Texas has suspended his license to practice, and he has been unable to negotiate a reasonable settlement of the debt. In David's words, "It doesn't make sense. It's almost like the government doesn't want me to practice medicine—never mind that it's the only way I can reasonably even have a shot at paying this mountain of money back!" David is currently driving trucks in Amarillo to make ends meet.

Then there's Tina Lutz, a single mother of two in Tupelo, Mississippi, who originally borrowed about six thousand dollars but now owes more than thirty-one thousand dollars. As a result of being hounded by collection companies, Tina has "been a nervous wreck for years" and is considering quitting her job and "dropping off the radar" in order to escape the relentless pressure put on her by various collection companies.

The student loans of Robert, an Air Force captain, defaulted in the mid-1990s while he was serving in the military. His original thirty-five thousand dollars in loans grew to a hundred and fifty-five thousand despite his efforts to negotiate with the lender, the Illinois Student Assistance Commission; they continue to demand payment in full. Like most StudentLoan Justice.org members, Robert absolutely agrees that he should pay what he owes, but he simply cannot deal with a debt of this magnitude.

The stories of citizens who've been hurt—and hurt badly—by their student loans are widespread. Personal accounts submitted to StudentLoanJustice.org range from relatively mild examples of borrowers who resent being held captive by their lenders due to the impossibility of refinancing their loans to extreme cases where citizens simply decided that life was not worth living under the weight of insurmountable student loan debt. Submissions from citizens who have been forced off the grid owing to the overwhelming escalation of their student loans are very common. Accounts from borrowers who have had Social Security or disability income taken from them are increasing. Citizens who have decided to leave the country because of their student loan debts are coming forward in increasing numbers. In this book, you will see the human face of this issue that affects all cultures, regions, professions, and ages.

The Solution

The current student loan system in this country works extremely well for banks and quite well for the federal government, but it has effectively crippled millions of Americans. Ironically, their attempts to achieve the American dream through higher education have turned their lives into living nightmares from which they have no recourse. Surely, the present-day scenario is not what President Johnson and the Congress of 1965 had in mind when they created the federal student loan system. Their intention was to assist Americans in bettering themselves, and thus the nation, through higher education; it was not to make them captive to an unethical financing system that penalizes the people who need aid most.

While experts on all sides of the student loan issue debate, conjecture, and argue about the best course forward for the student loan system, the most obvious solution is abundantly clear: it is imperative that standard consumer protections be returned to student loans.

Recent Legislation and Its Implications

The November 2006 change in political control in both the House and Senate certainly caused great concern for Sallie Mae, which had until then enjoyed unprecedented influence with both of these legislative bodies. The new Congress passed legislation that cut into the company's margins by reducing lender subsidies and decreasing interest rates for students, and in September 2007, it was signed into law by President Bush.

However, the change in the political wind only strengthened Sallie Mae's quest for dominance of the industry. On the morning of April 16, 2007, Sallie Mae announced that it had agreed to be acquired by John Christopher Flowers, a private equity magnate who was backed by student lenders JPMorgan Chase and the Bank of America. The acquisition of Sallie Mae by these banks—both among the top five student lenders in the country—seemed likely to increase the dominance of the new entity over the industry. Many of Sallie Mae's longtime shareholders saw this as an opportunity to cash out, and most sold their positions in Sallie Mae when the news was announced and the stock price of the company spiked.

The deal, it turns out, was short-lived. The legislation signed by the president in the fall of 2007 caused the investor consortium to have second thoughts about the acquisition. The private equity credit crunch that happened during the same time period, perhaps an additional factor, ultimately caused the J. C. Flowers group to pull out of the deal. Albert Lord, now Sallie Mae chairman, had intended to cash out and leave the company, but he was brought back in to help its severely stumbling stock price. Whether or not he will be successful remains to be seen.

While the legislation passed by the new Congress had some benefits for borrowers, the sorely needed consumer protections that had been stripped from student loans remain absent. The new financial pressures on the industry caused by this legislation and the credit market in general are likely to exacerbate the predatory collection activities being used against the borrowers. More than ever, Congress needs to restore these protections. It is my hope that this book will play some role in rousing the political fervor needed to achieve this goal.

CHAPTER TWO

Who Benefited

Since the 1970s, the burden of college tuition has shifted dramatically from the state to the student. In 1977, it is estimated that students and their families borrowed about $1.8 billion through U.S. federal loan programs in order to attend college. By 1989, this amount had increased to twelve billion dollars. By 1996, it had soared to thirty billion dollars.[1] Today, more than seventy billion dollars is borrowed through federal loan programs, and more than fifteen billion dollars is borrowed annually from private lenders.

Congress's removal of standard consumer protections for these loans, the growing tendency to attach fees to the debt, and the collection methods that student loan companies were allowed to use all set the stage for unprecedented profiteering by the lending industry. It is not surprising that many personal fortunes were made by well-connected student loan executives—particularly after the amendments to the Higher Education Act in 1998.

While the most startling wealth was accrued by executives and staff of the Sallie Mae Corporation and its subsidiaries, personal fortunes were also realized by a bevy of other student loan executives who worked at both nonprofit and for-profit student loan organizations. Certain elected officials also made large monetary gains as a result of their participation in the legislative efforts described previously. Key federal government employees—particularly those in the U.S. Department of Education—achieved significant personal gain because of this legislation and its administration.

Finally, universities and university officials profited tremendously from this legislation—and sometimes illegally. While this chapter focuses on a small group of individuals who did exceedingly well as a result of the new legislation, those few should by no means be considered a comprehensive overview.

Sallie Mae and Its Executives

Clearly, the single entity that realized the most financial gain from the amendments to the Higher Education Act is Sallie Mae. It is only natural that the chief architects of these legislative actions were also its chief beneficiaries. A simple glance at Sallie Mae's stock chart over the past decade as compared to standard stock-market indices for the same time period confirms the company's tremendous growth. It is very telling that its stock price actually accelerated in the aftermath of the dot-com recession. Indeed, between 1995 and 2000, Sallie Mae's stock price increased by nearly 1,700 percent.

Between 1997 and 2006, Sallie Mae's loan holdings grew from $45 billion to $123 billion. Note that from 2000 to 2005, Sallie Mae's loan holdings increased by about 86 percent, while its fee income far outpaced this growth, increasing by 228 percent during the same time period.[2] Albert Lord bragged in the 2003 Sallie Mae annual report that their record earnings were attributable in part to collections on defaulted loans.[3]

In 2005, *Fortune* magazine called Sallie Mae the second most profitable company (Microsoft was eighteenth on the list that year), and its CEO again topped the *Washington Post*'s list of highest paid CEOs in Washington, D.C. According to conservative estimates by Bethany McLean of *Fortune* magazine, Albert Lord had made in excess of $224 million dollars in compensation. An October 2007 article in the *New York Times* estimated that the total value of Lord's holdings in Sallie Mae exceeded $450 million.[4] *Fortune* reported that CEO Tim Fitzpatrick, who has since left the company, had made approximately $125 million in compensation.[5]

Albert Lord spent, or attempted to spend, his money in diverse ways. In early 2005, the *Washington Post* announced that an investment group he led had tendered an offer of perhaps $480 million to purchase the Washington, D.C., Major League Baseball team, the Washington Nationals.[6] (His bid was ultimately rejected.) In late 2005, Lord announced plans for the construction of a private luxury eighteen-hole golf course in Anne Arundel County, Maryland. Lord also used his money to become the largest donor to the campaign coffers of a number of politicians. In the 2004 election cycle, Lord, along with his wife, Suzanne, contributed more than $250,000 to various elected officials and political action committees. In addition, in what was seen by many as an attempt to ingratiate himself with Pennsylvania politicians so that they would help Sallie Mae's bid to acquire the state loan agency, Lord donated five million dollars to Penn State, his alma mater. He also donated money to state legislators in other key states where Sallie Mae had designs on loan agencies.

Probably the most compelling example of the wealth that Lord, Fitzpatrick, and other Sallie Mae executives received is the stock bonuses that the company reserved for employees once it went public, in March 2005. According to Sallie Mae filings with the Securities and Exchange Commission, the company set aside about $3.6 billion for stock offerings to its employees. On a per-employee basis, this is approximately $640,000 per person for the eight-year period beginning in 1997 (see appendix). How this wealth was distributed among Sallie Mae employees is unknown, but it is certainly likely that the majority of this wealth went to top management rather than to the rank-and-file employees.

Other Student Loan Organizations

While Sallie Mae executives amassed tremendous wealth as a result of congressional legislation, other individuals also made fortunes at the expense of students. The remainder of this chapter is devoted to other not-for-profit and for-profit companies and organizations that substantially benefited from the legislation.

Until now, there has been little discussion of student loan guarantors. Created in 1965 with the legislation of the Higher Education Act, student loan guarantors were originally designed to act along with the federal government as entities responsible for co-guaranteeing student loans, thus sharing the risk against default.

Over time, however, it became apparent that these guarantors were unwilling to share this risk. Bob Shireman, noted higher education expert, likened the relationship between the student loan guarantors and the federal government to that of bad roommates. According to Shireman, "The system is like a roommate who was supposed to split the rent but who you end up paying to live with you. Instead of reducing the federal costs as originally intended, guaranty agencies turned out to add yet another layer of subsidies and complexities to the system."[7]

In practice, student loan guarantors do two things. First, they extract significant funding from the federal government in return for serving in an extremely vague and ill-defined oversight capacity to the lenders. They themselves enjoy very little oversight from the federal government.

Second, they take defaulted student loan debt, attach massive penalties and fees to the debt, then proceed to use the various collection tools provided by the federal government to extract this increased amount from the borrower.

Mr. Shireman and others have noted that in an equitable world, the refusal of guarantor agencies to assume any risk in the student loan program should have taken them out of the game from the outset. Congress, however, kept sweetening the deal by offering additional subsidies, increased penalties and fees attached to the debt, and enhanced collection powers.

A good example of a guarantor gone awry is EdFund. EdFund was chartered with the State of California in 1997. Its 2005 mission statement defines EdFund's activities as "maximizing benefits to borrowers by being the premier service provider in the student loan industry." In actuality, this abstract mission statement serves only to conceal the true nature of the activities that the organization performs. Comprehensive analysis of Ed-Fund's IRS filings reveals that the organization has experienced explosive growth since its creation. From 1998 to 2003, its program revenue nearly doubled, going from fifty-five million dollars to ninety million dollars. Its salary expenditures similarly increased during that time period, and its executives received dramatic salary increases. President Becky Stilling's salary, for example, doubled over a three-year period, going from $127,000 to $263,000. Her counsel Wendie Doyle saw her pay rise from $36,000 in 2000 to $225,000 in 2003. Another VP's pay went from $99,000 in 1999 to $246,000 in 2003. Similar increases were found for other EdFund executives.[8]

Like Britt Napoli, Amy of Apple Valley can explain firsthand how EdFund makes its money. Amy originally borrowed forty-eight thousand dollars and later consolidated with Sallie Mae. Owing to a divorce and an extended period of unemployment, in 1997 Amy defaulted on her loans, and by 2005, the amount she owed had escalated, with penalties and fees, to over $118,000. EdFund was unwilling to negotiate with Amy on the reduction of this debt.

Desperate to put an end to her defaulted loan with EdFund, in 2005 Amy refinanced her home and placed well over a hundred thousand dollars in escrow for EdFund. EdFund refused her payment, claiming that her balance was actually higher, and instead began garnishing her wages. According to Amy, "It was as if they didn't want me to pay this debt off. Knowing that I had assets, they just sat on it for as long as possible to make additional interest and these collection fees."

Another example of the personal fortunes that are made by executives of student loan guarantors is the case of the USA Group in Fishers, Indiana, formed as a nonprofit in 1986. Their mission statement:

"USA Group Loan Services, Inc., provides data processing, collection, and other loan servicing for over 4 million loans to over 1.7 million students and their parents. USA Group Loan Services services these loans to ensure they are in compliance with the regulations as established by Congress under the Higher Education Act of 1965, as amended."

Like Sallie Mae, this organization, headed until 2001 by James Lintzenich, spent millions lobbying Congress, and its "part-time" executives donated large amounts to elected officials and PACs. Part-time CEO (and chairman of the board) Lintzenich saw his salary increase from $613,000 in 1997 to over $3.5 million in 2000. The part-time chief operating officer and president Andrew Lynch saw a one-year increase in salary from $173,000 in 1999 to over $1.4 million in 2000. EdFund was not an isolated example; increases in salary were demonstrated across the board for the USA Group.

The USA Group was acquired by Sallie Mae in 2000; its board of directors and its executive staff were *the same people*. Shortly thereafter, Sallie Mae paid off key employees of the USA Group with an amount totaling fifty million dollars. Lintzenich resigned nine months after the acquisition, as did other USA Group executives. Mr. Lintzenich received twenty-one million dollars in stock after the buyout, a salary increase of well over four million dollars, and he received an early exit payoff of five million dollars from Sallie Mae, a stipulation that was written into his contract in the event that he left Sallie Mae within one year of the buyout. He also received a $530,000-per-year retirement package.[9]

USA Group Salaries

	2000	1999	1998	1997
James Lintzenich (part-time chairman and CEO)	$3,518,868	$883,652	$747,970	$613,510
Andrew Lynch (part-time president and COO)	$1,470,610	$173,750		
Jeffrey Good (part-time VP and CFO)	$799,289	$193,048		
Robert Grennee, Jr. (part-time senior VP)	$381,261	$285,050		
Martha Lamkin (part-time VP)	$859,988	$448,636	$356,241	$327,323
June McCormack (part-time VP)	$834,762	$450,776	$173,498	
Carl Dalstrom (part-time VP)	$686,869	$386,740	$293,971	

Executive Compensation for the USA Group

Since 1997, Sallie Mae has purchased a disturbing number of other nonprofit student loan guarantors—including Nellie Mae (1999), NELA (2000), and Southwest Student Loan Services (2001)—and as a result, many student loan executives found themselves exceedingly rich.

Elected Officials

Sallie Mae and others in the industry attempted to change student loan legislation, and they certainly used every strategy at their disposal. As a result, the campaign coffers of key legislators were handsomely filled. Indeed, of the Education Committee members in the 109th Congress, sixteen out of the seventeen senators and thirty-seven out of the fifty-one House representatives received donations from the Sallie Mae PAC. However, the funds for the Sallie Mae PAC had a much wider distribution

than just these two committees. While the legality of these lobbying efforts is not being argued here, it is instructive to note
where those lobbying dollars went. For example, the top two
recipients of Sallie Mae PAC funds were John Boehner and
Howard "Buck" McKeon, each of whom had served as chairman of the House Education Committee. It has been found that
family members of key legislators, including Boehner and
McKeon, benefited financially from the student loan industry,
through jobs working directly for student loan companies
and through the donations given by student loan interests to
PACs and campaign committees.

In 2007, citizen activists from StudentLoanJustice.org publicly called for members of both the House and Senate Education
Committees to cease taking political contributions from student
loan interests.[10] However, these calls went largely unheeded.
The details regarding financial benefits for family members
raises serious questions about, at the very least, these legislators'
abilities to make unbiased policy decisions regarding higher education laws.

Senator Mike Enzi

In October 2006, StudentLoanJustice.org uncovered interesting
lobbying activities regarding a group called the Making Business
Excel political action committee.

This PAC was led by Danielle Enzi (its treasurer). Mrs. Enzi's
father-in-law, Michael Enzi, is a U.S. senator and at the time was
chairman of the Senate Education Committee (Health, Education, Labor, and Pensions). According to the Federal Elections
Commission, as of October 14, 2006, this political action committee had received a total of $504,592 but had only paid out
about a hundred thousand dollars in campaign contributions.
A portion of its operating expenses, $121,000, went to a firm
called Enzi Strategies, LLC. Other expenses included chartered
jets, fishing trips, and thousand-dollar lunches.

Of the twenty highest individual contributions given to this PAC in the 2006 election cycle, thirteen came from executives of Sallie Mae, Nelnet, education lobbyists, and colleges. This includes donations from the chairman, CEO, and several VPs of Sallie Mae. Fifty-two of the total 134 individual donations came from executives of Sallie Mae, Nelnet, their lobbyists, and other persons with a professional interest in higher education financing.

When *Fortune* magazine questioned these activities, Senator Enzi's staff responded that "Senator Enzi's actions are driven by what he believes to be the best interests of the people of Wyoming."[11]

Congressman Howard "Buck" McKeon

Congressman Buck McKeon was chairman of the House Education Committee until 2007; he and John Boehner were prime sponsors of the Higher Education Amendments of 1997. McKeon's wife, Patricia, ran his campaign committee during the 2006 election cycle. It took in nearly a million dollars during this time and paid out about six hundred thousand dollars to candidates, with about four hundred thousand going to operating expenses. Most of the campaign's payments were not itemized, but it was found that Patricia had taken well over a hundred and fifty thousand dollars in salary from the PAC. Most of the largest donors to this PAC were student loan interests, including Sallie Mae, Nelnet, and Corinthian Colleges.

Congressman John Boehner

From 2001 to 2006, Congressman Boehner was chairman of the House Education Committee. During this time, he was by far the largest recipient of campaign contributions from student loan interests. Although Congressman Boehner described himself as being a champion of free markets, his actions on behalf of the largest lenders—Sallie Mae and Citibank—served chiefly to shut out competition in the industry and protect the profits of the largest lenders.

In December 2004, Mr. Boehner attended a benefit hosted by Sallie Mae vice president Rose DiNapoli and the Consumer Bankers Association. At the dinner, which was attended by executives who'd each paid a thousand dollars a ticket, Boehner told the crowd, "Know that I hold you in my trusted hands, I have enough rabbits up my sleeve to be able to get where we need to." Shortly thereafter, on December 26, language was inserted into an education bill that helped the biggest lenders tremendously in their quest to stave off competition. Simply put, Mr. Boehner was instrumental in upholding the single-holder rule. The single-holder rule was legislation passed on behalf of the big lenders; it required that students who consolidated their loans after graduating had to do so with the same companies that had originally made the loans. This legislation was obviously bad for competition. It was repealed in 2006, but refinancing previously consolidated student loans remains impossible for most borrowers.

This was not an isolated case. Mr. Boehner and Mr. McKeon were both instrumental in shutting down the Super Two-Step, the loophole through which students were able to refinance their student loans under better terms or rates or both. According to Marcus Katz, the retired student loan executive who started the Educational Loan Administration Group (ELA) and who fought for competition in the industry, "It was pretty clear that Congress would listen only to the Sallie Maes and the Citibanks. If it was anti-competitive legislation the big guys wanted, then that's what they got. Too bad for the small guys. Too bad for competition."[12]

Stephen Koff at the *Cleveland Plain Dealer* reported that during a 2001 golf game with an executive, Mr. Boehner had sought

—and found—a job for his daughter at the student loan collection company General Revenue Corporation (GRC). GRC was purchased by Sallie Mae in 2002.

Sallie Mae provided private jets to congresspersons on a regular basis, flew legislators to Boca Raton for golf outings, and contributed two hundred and fifty thousand dollars to President George Bush for the 2004 election cycle. After the majority-changing congressional elections of 2006, CEO Tim Fitzpatrick vowed to "work both sides of the aisle"—all for the benefit of members of Congress, most notably those who sat on House and Senate Education Committees. In the 110th Congress of 2006, Sallie Mae contributed to the campaigns of thirty-three of the forty-nine members of the House Education Committee and seventeen of the twenty-one member of the Senate Education Committee.

University and College Financial Aid Administrators

The largest beneficiaries of the changes in the HEA over the years have probably been colleges and universities. Over the past three decades, the cost of attending college has skyrocketed; on average, tuition costs have risen at more than double the rate of inflation. This increase has been borne largely by the students in the form of student loans. As mentioned previously, today's undergraduate student borrower leaves school with more than twenty thousand dollars in student loan debt, and the typical graduate student leaves owing more than forty-two thousand dollars. This does not include other types of debt (credit cards, for example).

One need only visit the local university and witness the brand-new gyms, libraries, elaborate student centers, and other brick-and-mortar projects to see that colleges have flourished over the last few decades. More to the point, in 2007 the *Chronicle of Higher Education* reported that after being adjusted for inflation, the salaries of university presidents were at record levels.

One telling statistic: in 2000, only about twelve private university presidents earned more than five hundred thousand dollars a year; in 2006, there were more than double that number, twenty-seven.

To be sure, in recent decades, universities have walked in lockstep with the student loan interests. In fact, it is often impossible to distinguish between the two. From lobbying activities on the Hill to call-center operations on university campuses, colleges and student lenders often occupied the same space, both figuratively and, unfortunately, literally.

In 2006, the New York State attorney general Eliot Spitzer started an investigation into student loan companies' relationships with universities, and the results of the examination, which was completed by his immediate successor, Andrew Cuomo, were shocking. It was found that universities were profiting tremendously from their relationships with student loan companies, and that in exchange for being on the universities' preferred-lenders list, the student loan companies were involved in many illegal financial transactions. Moreover, universities were ceding control of their operations to these companies.

Specifically, student loan companies had established financial aid hotlines in the names of the universities, and when they answered calls from students they claimed to be representatives of the universities; in fact, they were nothing more than salespeople attempting to get students to sign with their particular loan companies.

In the first half of 2007, the New York attorney general's investigation made headlines, and this spawned additional research, most notably by the New America Foundation. The findings showed that not only did colleges and universities enjoy illegal, unethical, collusive relationships with student loan companies, but some financial aid administrators actually held direct financial stakes in the very same lenders that they were promoting on campus. A few specific examples include:

- **Johns Hopkins University**—Ellen Frishberg, director of
  financial aid at Johns Hopkins, received over $155,000
  from various student loan entities, including Student Loan
  Xpress, Collegiate Funding Services, the U.S. Department
  of Education, Campus Direct, American Express, Student
  Loan Processors, KnowledgeFirst, Higher Education
  Washington, Inc., and Global Student Loan Corporation.
  She maintains that the money paid to her did not induce
  bias, although Student Loan Xpress was prominent on
  the Johns Hopkins preferred-lender list.
- **Columbia University**—David Charlow, financial aid
  director of Columbia University in 2003, owned at least
  seventy-five hundred shares of Student Loan Xpress,
  worth approximately seventy-two thousand dollars at the
  time of the proffered sale.
- **University of Texas at Austin**—Lawrence Burt, associate
  vice president and director of student financial aid at the
  university, was found to have owned fifteen hundred
  shares in Student Loan Xpress; he sold them in 2005.
- **University of Southern California**—Catherine Thomas,
  financial aid director at the University of Southern California, owned fifteen hundred shares in Student Loan Xpress.
  It has not been ascertained when and for how much
  Ms. Thomas sold her shares.

Former Department of Labor secretary Robert Reich correctly
predicted in April 2007 that the malfeasances that had emerged
up to that point were only the tip of a scandalous iceberg.[13]
Indeed, a cavalcade of other inappropriate, even illegal, activities have been discovered since that time. These are detailed in
chapter 6.

While the individuals mentioned above have subsequently
left their jobs, and many universities have signed ethics agreements since the investigation results were made public, the

influence of student loan companies on campus remains strong. Universities still engage in school-as-lender, opportunity funds, and other arrangements that essentially come down to the lender paying the school based on the number of students the school sends its way. Also, many—if not most—universities allow student loan companies and organizations funded by student loan companies to perform the students' entrance and exit loan counseling. This is seen by many to be an opportunity for the student lenders to market their products to students. (Why else would the lenders be willing to perform these services for no cost?) Further, professional financial aid administrators' organizations, such as the Rocky Mountain Association of Student Financial Aid Administrators, continue to allow student loan executives on their boards and solicit the bulk of their funding from student lenders.

The U.S. Department of Education

While the U.S. Department of Education pays lenders, guarantors, and collection companies billions every year in federal subsidies, one overlooked and underreported fact is that the U.S. Department of Education actually *makes* money from defaulted student loans. In 2004, John Hechinger of the *Wall Street Journal* reported that for defaulted loans, every dollar of principal is reclaimed and an additional 20 percent in interest and fees is realized in the form of payments by the borrowers. This is over and above the profits that the guarantors and collection companies take from the borrowers to begin with.

In fall 2006, the Office of the Inspector General warned Theresa Shaw, the head of the Office of Federal Student Aid for the Department of Education, that a recent OIG report stated that her oversight program for student loans was highly vulnerable to conflicts of interest and that the department relied too heavily on "partnerships" with student loan companies rather than real oversight.[14] Shaw had been brought into the department directly from Sallie Mae, where she had been a vice president.

The New America Foundation discovered in the spring of 2007 that a key employee of the Department of Education actually held stock in a student loan company that he was charged with overseeing. Matteo Fontana, they reported, had held stock in Student Loan Xpress during his tenure at the U.S. Department of Education; he had profited roughly a hundred thousand dollars from this, which he'd failed to disclose to the department. Fontana, also a former Sallie Mae employee, had been appointed by Theresa Shaw to manage the Financial Partners division of the Office of Federal Student Aid—the very division that the Office of the Inspector General had warned Ms. Shaw about the previous year.

Shaw has since left the U.S. Department of Education, and Fontana has been placed on administrative leave, but a number of unanswered questions remain. For instance, how many other Department of Education employees held or are holding stock in student loan companies? Are there other illegal activities occurring within the Department of Education, violations that can't be found by outside groups going through public documents? These questions cry out for investigation.

Clearly, the changes in higher education policy in the United States and the actions of those who sought to profit from them has enriched a relatively small number of entities and individuals—often through illegal, corrupt, and collusive relationships perpetuated over long periods of time. Indeed, student loans have become the most lucrative and, simultaneously, the most oppressive and predatory loan instrument in our nation's history. This has contributed to the unprecedented escalation in the cost of college tuition and to the unbearable hardships of those struggling to repay their loans.

CHAPTER THREE

Collection Abuses

"I knew there was something fishy going on with Sallie Mae... it's called fraud. It's definitely highway robbery."

"No one stops these people and they stop at nothing to extort millions from the public."

These allegations—and more like them—have been received by StudentLoanJustice.org from citizens across the country. However, the people making these allegations are neither angry borrowers nor student advocates. They are current and former employees of student loan companies.

Since 1998, defaulted loans have become lucrative for all concerned except, of course, the borrowers. An entire industry devoted to collecting the penalties and fees over and above the original debt has sprung up around them. In fact, it is far more profitable for the industry when students default on their debts than when they pay the loans back on time. This is because when a loan is defaulted, not only is the lender paid nearly the full balance of the loan (both principal and interest), but the guarantors of the loan and the collection companies they contract with— which are often owned by the original lenders—can still collect on the defaulted loan, the amount of which is now vastly inflated by fees and accrued interest.

In 1998, Congress removed standard consumer protections from student loans. Combine that with the collection tools Congress gave to the industry—such as administrative wage and tax-return garnishment (for which no court order is needed), Social Security and disability garnishment, and suspension of state licenses—and one can see how the industry might find the prospect of student loan default quite appealing. Indeed, it was estimated by CBS News that this income accounted for about one fifth of Sallie Mae's revenue.[1]

Evidence of the extreme profitability of delinquent student loan debt is clear, convincing, and widespread. Since the 1998 legislation, Sallie Mae acquired some of the largest student loan collection companies in the nation, thereby ensuring that this secondary source of income would go to the company. In the company's 2003 annual report, CEO Albert Lord stated that the company's record-breaking profits were attributable to two sources: loan originations and *collections on defaulted loans.* Sallie Mae's fee income increased by about 228 percent between 2000 and 2005, while, according to their 2004 annual report, its loan portfolio grew by only about 87 percent during the same time period.

By 1998, there was a perverse financial incentive for the student loan servicing companies to do a horrible job of loan administration. The more ineffective the companies' customer service was, the more likely it became that students would default—and thus, the more money the student loan companies would ultimately make.

It is no secret within the industry that the collection powers it has been afforded are without rival. Stories of senior citizens having their Social Security income taken, people with terminal illnesses having their disability income attached, members of the working poor having their wages garnished—usually just to cover fees and interest on their debts—are widespread. However, recent evidence suggests that the collection industry has superseded even those powers provided by Congress for collecting on student loans; it has engaged in widespread abuse and taken outright fraudulent actions against borrowers.

In April of 2007, Edward Kennedy, the chairman of the Senate Health, Education, Labor, and Pensions Committee, launched an investigation based on reports the committee had received from individual borrowers, many of whom had also submitted stories to StudentLoanJustice.org. This chapter describes some of the abuses that have already been documented and covers some of the stories that were used as the basis for the Senate investigation. Comments from lender employees that were submitted to the StudentLoanJustice.org Web site are also detailed here; they give strong support to the notion that the industry actually induces borrowers to default.

Sallie Mae and Others Making False Claims

In 2001, the Office of the Inspector General announced that Sallie Mae had agreed to pay $3.4 million to settle a case in which the company had been found to be defaulting loans and submitting them for government payments when in actuality no efforts had been made to collect on the debt. According to documents released by the Department of Justice, a Sallie Mae employee created false records indicating that borrowers had been contacted or that reasonable attempts to contact the borrowers had been made when no such events had occurred.[2]

Even more disturbing, this type of collection abuse was not limited to Sallie Mae but was found across the industry. In 1998, it was reported that a Florida company, Cybernetics and Systems, Inc., had similarly made false claims about contacting and attempting to contact thousands of borrowers. The firm pleaded guilty to fraud charges and was assessed thirty million dollars in penalties and restitution.[3]

In October 2000, Corus Bank of Chicago agreed to settle similar claims made by the Office of the Inspector General. Like Sallie Mae, Corus had submitted claims for guaranty payments to the U.S. government when no efforts had been made to collect on the loans. In this case, the Corus manager in charge of student loans had fabricated evidence to show that the borrowers had been contacted when in fact they had not. Thousands of loans had been illegally defaulted by Corus, and the value of the settlement was estimated to be over eleven million dollars.[4]

While these and similar cases have grabbed headlines, one wonders what happened to the borrowers. The borrowers whose loans were illegally placed into default were subjected to the overwhelming consequences typical of defaulted loans. Although the federal government—at least in these cases—was able to recover its losses, nothing has been found regarding restitution or compensation, monetary or otherwise, made to the borrowers these crimes affected. Furthermore, one has to wonder how many other instances of this type of fraud exist in the industry today and how many lives have been ruined as a result.

Dustin Logan of Amarillo, Texas, can attest firsthand to the questionable administration of Corus Bank. Mr. Logan, who in the late 1980s borrowed about seventy-five hundred dollars, was found to be suffering from a form of autism that prevented him from obtaining gainful employment. He was declared totally and permanently disabled by the Social Security Administration—one of the few conditions sufficient to qualify for the discharge of student loans. According to Mr. Logan, he submitted the necessary paperwork to Corus Bank, and he was told that everything was taken care of. He remembers clearly the conversation he had with the bank officer in 1995; the officer assured Mr. Logan that the discharge paperwork was in his hands. According to Mr. Logan, "He finished with the encouraging words 'You're all set.'" Logan wonders what more he could have done.

That was the last time Mr. Logan ever interacted with Corus Bank—he assumed that his loans had been dismissed, and he moved on with his life. Then, in 1999, he began receiving threatening phone calls from EdFund, a student loan guarantor in California. EdFund was demanding immediate payment of approximately twenty thousand dollars. Dustin tried to explain that he suffered from a total and permanent disability, but according to him, "To my shock, they refused to listen. I then tried to send them copies of my disability paperwork, but they refused to accept them. To say that I was guilty until proven innocent would be an understatement. I was considered guilty, period, with no rights to present my own defense. Corus had claimed that I had never filed for disability, and that was the only testimony that EdFund would accept."

Unable to convince EdFund to consider his plight, Mr. Logan contacted Congressman Mac Thornberry's office. According to Logan, "The congressman's people danced around the issue for a year and a half. They made only a token effort of writing letters, which never amounted to anything. Basically, they simply accepted whatever EdFund claimed, despite the fact that I had proof contradicting EdFund's statements."

After learning of the false-claim charges against Corus Bank, Mr. Logan decided to try once again to get some help from Congressman Thornberry's office, hoping that the suit might convince them to revisit his case. According to Logan, "I couldn't have been more wrong. Once again, the lady started screaming into the phone. She literally would not let me speak. She kept shouting louder and louder, 'This is your fault! You dropped the ball!' Then, when she finally ran out of breath, she simply hung up on me. I never had a chance to present my evidence."

To date, Logan has gotten nowhere despite his repeated efforts. "This nightmare has continued ever since; nine long years. In that time, I have been harassed by one collection agency after another. It just keeps getting worse and worse. In fact, now, the threatening phone calls are literally coming every day, often twice or three times a day."

Abusing the Borrowers

One does not need to go far to find evidence of bad customer service and even illegal collection tactics in the student loan industry. This seems to be particularly true for Sallie Mae and its subsidiaries. On January 25, 2007, the attorney general of Illinois filed a lawsuit against one of Sallie Mae's subsidiaries, Arrow Financial Services, LLC. The suit alleged that the company violated the Illinois Consumer Fraud and Deceptive Practices Act and the federal Fair Debt Collections Practices Act. Interestingly, the lawsuit alleged that as of the time of filing, 660 complaints against Arrow Financial had been received by the Illinois attorney general, and more than eight hundred complaints against them had been filed with the Better Business Bureau.[5]

While nonprofit guaranty agencies are exempt from the provisions of the Fair Debt Collection Practices Act, for-profit collection companies are not. The provisions of this act prohibit collectors from misrepresentation, fraud, false claims, and other tactics that can be used to pressure borrowers. Nonetheless, StudentLoanJustice.org has received hundreds of submissions from borrowers who have compelling accounts of being subjected to illegal collection tactics at the hands of unethical collection companies.

Many borrowers tell of their loans being defaulted either without their being contacted by the student loan companies, much like in the false-claims cases described above, or despite their concerted efforts to maintain the loans in good standing through deferments and forbearances. Borrowers frequently complain that they send in forms to the lenders and guarantors only to have the companies claim that the forms were never received or were lost.

Several of the submissions detail stories of collection agents lying to the borrowers. In many cases, the collectors claimed to be employees of the U.S. Department of Education. Another common ploy is for the collector to call the borrower's employer in an attempt to establish an administrative wage garnishment, warning the employer that withholding information about the borrower could result in criminal prosecution, fines, and even jail time.

One StudentLoanJustice.org member from Missouri, who reports that his original fourteen thousand dollars in loans has exploded to about forty-eight thousand dollars, states, "I could write a book on the underhanded activities of the Dept. of Ed.'s collection agencies. I think I have been through at least ten. They have called my employer, misrepresented themselves as a credit card or loan company or told them I didn't pay my debts; they have called my neighbors, misrepresenting themselves as a parcel delivery service; they have screamed at me on the phone, insulted my character, have called me lazy, called me a liar . . . the list goes on."

The borrower continues: "I have tried a countless number of times to make payment arrangements, but none of the collection agencies will accept a 'reasonable and affordable' payment plan. They all state it is not reasonable to accept fifty dollars a month on a balance such as mine. They misplace the paperwork, become rude, and as soon as they figure out they can make no money off of me they discontinue working on my account and pass me on to the next collection agency, where the process begins all over again."

The borrower says he was never informed about income-contingent repayment options. He writes:

I recently discovered they are required by law to accept a "reasonable and affordable" payment amount. Guess what? No Dept. of Ed. collection agency I have spoken with in the last twelve years obeys that law. None. They are out to make money on the collection—period—with no regard whatsoever to the consumer or the laws of the United States. Had the collection agency I spoke with ten to twelve years ago obeyed the law, I probably wouldn't have a student loan debt. I could have made my income-contingent payments, went back to school and finished my education, and paid off all my debt. Instead, they have created a no-win situation out of pure greed and unscrupulous tactics.

The complaints described by this borrower are extremely common among StudentLoanJustice.org members. Any one of hundreds of submissions telling this same story could have been substituted for this one. Reports of being misled, lied to, threatened, and harassed are the rule rather than the exception. (Readers are encouraged to visit the StudentLoanJustice.org Web site to read similar accounts from across the country.)

It is understandable that one might be skeptical of the actual facts of the matter when reading borrower accounts of collection abuses. However, allegations of serious collection abuses have come not only from borrowers but also from subcontractors and employees within the industry. These allegations mirror those made by borrowers and are described below.

Contractors from the Inside Speak Out

Premiere Credit of North America, LLC, is a self-styled shark of the student loan collection business. Indeed, Premiere's corporate headquarters houses a four-thousand-gallon shark tank in its lobby. The company proudly displays the shark tank on the home page of its corporate Web site, claiming that these predators have "qualities that Premiere Credit of North America nurtures as a part of its corporate culture."[6]

In February 2007, StudentLoanJustice.org received a submission from Joseph Leal, president of U.S. Recoveries Worldwide, a small debt-collection company that until recently had been under contract to collect debt for Premiere Credit. U.S. Recoveries' employees had been monitored by auditors from the U.S. Department of Education and been found to have committed violations of the Fair Debt Collection Practices Act. However, according to Mr. Leal, these employees had been on the job for less than a month and had received all of their training for student loan debt collection from the Premiere staff.

Mr. Leal described what he called "serious and egregious violations of the Fair Debt Collection and Practices Act." He alleged that his employees had been trained to misrepresent themselves as employees of the U.S. Department of Education. Mr. Leal noted that his employees had been told to threaten debtors and their families with prosecution and incarceration in order to collect on the debt. In addition, his employees had been trained to speak about the borrowers' defaulted loans with third parties, including members of the borrowers' families and their acquaintances. He stated that the company often used telephone technology that disguised the true origin of the calls and gave borrowers the impression that they were being called by relatives, state unemployment departments, and other sources.

Finally, Mr. Leal said that Premiere Credit was manipulating payments from the borrowers in violation of their signed agreements, exacting large down payments from them and then applying these payments against future installments so that the company could be paid more quickly from the contract—a practice that Mr. Leal said was found to be a serious violation of the FDCPA. Unfortunately, according to Mr. Leal, telephone records that may contain evidence of these violations are being deleted by Premiere Credit.

His company's brief contract with Premiere Credit gave Mr. Leal a glimpse of what goes on in the student loan collection industry, and he is appalled. "We have done collections for some big industries and various government agencies, and I can tell you, student loan collections are like none other. I could write a book on the various illegal activities I have witnessed in this industry. They do things that no other industry could get away with."

Don Gilbert, a typesetter in California, had a run-in with Premiere Credit that cost him significantly. The school that Gilbert attended, the Computer Learning Center, closed in January 2001, while Gilbert was still a student there. The guarantor of his loans, EdFund, refused an in-person hearing with Mr. Gilbert and instead passed the loans to Premiere Credit for collection. What happened next was, in Mr. Gilbert's word, *atrocious*. "Premiere Credit of North America used information that I provided Ed-Fund in anticipation of an in-person hearing; [they went] online and used my personal information (name, address, and Social Security number) to apply for an income-contingent debt consolidation loan from the Direct Loan Program. They made a repayment plan selection, supposedly on my behalf, but without my knowledge or consent."

To date, Mr. Gilbert says he has attempted "at least ten times" to have his loan discharged, since the school closed and filed for bankruptcy before he could complete his classes, but he has been unsuccessful. EdFund has refused to process his discharge, claiming that he graduated on January 25, 2001, although according to Mr. Gilbert, the school closed on January 21, 2001. His credit record has been damaged, and his life has been in limbo for more than five years. In his view, he has been the victim of criminally bad loan administration, numerous violations of the Fair Debt Collection and Practices Act, and fraud on the part of Premiere Credit.

Former Sallie Mae Employee Speaks Out

In August 2005, StudentLoanJustice.org received a submission from a former Sallie Mae employee. This employee was terminated after she'd worked in the collection department for four months. The events that led to her termination, according to her, involved a borrower who had paid his loan in full yet was still being billed. The borrower contacted her, not understanding why he was still being billed for his loan. He faxed copies of the canceled checks, and the employee verified in the phone log that the canceled checks (which had been cashed by Sallie Mae two months earlier) matched the paid-in-full amount. Confused, she asked her manager for guidance. According to her, "All my supervisor could tell me was to give this guy the runaround and end the call."

She continues, "This whole incident put a red flag in my head. When I received another call that same day regarding a similar incident, a huge red banner went up in my mind. I knew there was something fishy going on with Sallie Mae . . . it's called fraud. It's definitely highway robbery. Within a week, I was fired for having too much knowledge." The employee was sufficiently troubled by this incident to contact the first borrower's family and offer to help them in any legal proceedings. She says that the family did indeed pursue a legal case against Sallie Mae, and eventually the company had to pay them the original balance of the loan, plus damages.

Employees of Other Student Loan Companies Speak Out

While Sallie Mae, EdFund, and Premiere Credit seem to appear on the radar screen more often than other lenders, guarantors, and collection companies, they are by no means the only ones. In fact, StudentLoanJustice.org has received reports alleging serious misconduct by nearly every lender, guarantor, and collection company in the nation. Taken together, they paint a shocking picture of the state of the student loan industry.

A submission received in December 2007 from an employee of the Kentucky Higher Education Assistance Authority goes a long way toward proving this point. This employee, who has worked in both default collection and default prevention within the organization, wrote:

I am disgusted at what I see. The Sallie Mae model has taken over our management and now every huckster from around the world wants to be a Sallie Mae CEO. No one stops these people and they stop at nothing to extort millions from the public.

In eight years we have gone from a wholesome public venture to a loan-shark operation, preying on students who do not belong in college in the first place. Our VP of Asset Management comes from Providian Credit Card Co. and has single-handedly turned our agency into a big payday-advance type operation, preying on the old, minorities, anyone who is unable to stand up for themselves. I've seen greed destroy American higher education firsthand. The mafia would blush if they saw how our operation was run from the inside out.

This employee continues in subsequent e-mails:

Envy/greed run hand in hand. People I work with see what the CEO of Sallie Mae "earned" and now they are all greedy. They have forgotten the schools, students, lenders, employees. We have a rash of private people wanting entrance to this industry purely for a profit motive. It's a mess. Not sure what else I can say—a significant percentage of our portfolio is what I refer to as "sub-prime." Ninja loans, if you will. Our previous CEO targeted the poorest areas of Kentucky and Alabama, knowing that many if not all of these students would end up paying us large default collection fees over the long haul.

According to this employee, the company also engaged in egregious collection practices. He gave an example:

When I worked default collections, I refused to garnish a little old lady's disability check. Sweetest little old black lady you ever want to meet. She came with her son from Chicago so her son could play ball at the University of Kentucky—she signed a bunch of PLUS loans. She was eating a mac and cheese diet on her disability check and I received an order to garnish her rather than set up a low payment based on income. That's when I snapped and realized no one is protecting the public anymore.

The Senate Takes Notice

The 2007 change in the leadership of the Senate Health, Education, Labor, and Pensions (HELP) Committee was significant. The new chairman, Edward Kennedy, said that the nation ought to "get the money changers out of the temple, in terms of student loans."[7] True to his word, Kennedy tasked the HELP staff with a number of investigations, one regarding misconduct between lenders and universities and another regarding collection abuses within the industry.

As a result of interviews with borrowers across the country—many of whom were StudentLoanJustice.org members—the committee issued letters to both Sallie Mae and Nelnet (the owner of Premiere Credit). According to the letter to Sallie Mae, evidence had been found that indicated the company had engaged in the following activities:

- Telling a borrower's spouse that the borrower would go to jail if he didn't pay—a blatantly false assertion;
- Putting a borrower into default who lost his home in a natural disaster, adding substantial default and collection fees to his loan balance, taking tax refunds, and garnishing his wages—all in violation of guidance from the secretary of education;
- Harassing a widower about illegitimate, forged loans under the name of his deceased spouse;
- Refusing to negotiate with borrowers about deferment;
- Regularly calling borrowers at their job after being instructed to stop;

- Harassing borrowers' neighbors, family, and coworkers;
- Using abusive and profane language to intimidate borrowers;
- Attempting to collect debts not owed;
- Attempting to collect from deceased borrowers' families and relatives;
- Attempting to collect from elderly, disabled borrowers;
- Firing employees who attempt to help borrowers obtain correct information about their loan status;
- Instructing employees to give borrowers "the runaround" rather than provide them with correct information on their loan status; and
- Intentionally sending loan payment notices to an incorrect address in order to force a borrower's account into default.[8]

The chairman of Nelnet received a similar letter stating that information had been uncovered that indicated his company had refused to provide loan payment and history information to defaulted borrowers and had inappropriately consolidated borrowers' loans without the borrowers' consents.

This investigation is ongoing, and results have not yet been released. The fact that Senator Kennedy undertook this investigation is highly encouraging for the borrowers, and time will tell what the outcome will be. It is hoped that in the future this investigation will expand to ask other highly significant questions, such as whether the lenders have made concerted efforts to induce students to default on their loans.

There is another hugely important wrinkle that has developed in this debate. Over the past decade, lenders, guarantors, universities, and even the U.S. Department of Education have repeatedly pronounced that student loan defaults are decreasing. In December 2007, evidence emerged that, in fact, the opposite may be true.

In June 2006, the National Center for Education Statistics

released a study of a number of 1993 college graduates. Shockingly, the report found that 9.6 percent of the borrowers it had followed had defaulted on student loans within the first decade after graduation.[9] This was far higher than the cohort default rate that the industry frequently points to as evidence that defaults are decreasing. For graduates who had borrowed more than fifteen thousand dollars, the ten-year default rate was found to be nearly 20 percent. While this is alarming enough, Educationsector.org, a nonprofit think tank, used the same data the NCES report had used and found that for African Americans, the ten-year default rate was nearly double the overall rate—about 40 percent.[10]

In December 2007, the U.S. Department of Education released more current default data. The data showed that the five-year default rate for students leaving school in 2002 was 10.6 percent—this is higher than the ten-year default rate in the previous study.[11] While these data cannot easily be compared (the 1993 students' study looked at a relatively small sample and included graduates of four-year colleges only), there is compelling evidence that defaults are not decreasing but rising, and perhaps significantly.

If this proves to be the case, then one of the major arguments used to gather support for the federal student loan program is invalid. Furthermore, given the fact that collection companies, guarantors, and even the U.S. Department of Education actually make—not lose—money on defaulted loans, evidence that the default rate is increasing strengthens the argument that those organizations that are making money from defaulted loans may be the very entities responsible for their increase. Those whose loans were put into default despite their best efforts will have good reason to demand new legislation that finally provides justice for borrowers.

CHAPTER FOUR

The Borrowers

The debate over student loans continues, and much of the attention is focused on the culpability of the lenders. However, all too often, the plight of the borrowers hurt by the student loan system goes unnoticed. This chapter shares their stories so the reader can appreciate the depth and breadth of this problem.

Borrowers with student loan difficulties come in all ages, races, and fields of study. While there is no average borrower, a typical scenario is illustrated by Robert, who lives in California. In the late 1980s, he borrowed forty-two thousand dollars in undergraduate and graduate school loans, all of which were guaranteed by the federal government. His loans included funds for law school, but because of poor grades, he could not graduate. As a result, he was unable to obtain a good job, and he ended up defaulting on the debt shortly after leaving school. The loans were referred to Sallie Mae for collection.

Robert rehabilitated his loans in the 1990s and has made the monthly payments faithfully ever since. Nonetheless, today his balance is forty-five thousand dollars. He can only afford to pay the interest (9.5 percent), which totals almost $450 a month. He says, "At this rate, I will pay Sallie Mae for the rest of my life, at a whopping total that is many multiples of the original loans." So far, he has repaid more than fifty thousand dollars, but the amount of the principal is virtually unchanged.

Like most borrowers, Robert hadn't been aware of the lack of consumer protections behind this type of debt. "I did not know then, but I know now that I am precluded from discharging this debt through bankruptcy. Also, the rate for new loans is much lower than 9 percent. I feel that I should be able to refinance at the rate for new loans, but apparently this is not possible." He continues, "This is not nickel-and-dime stuff. It is strangling my life."

Robert was never able to capitalize on his education. Of course, he was nonetheless obligated to repay his loans. Because he was financially unable to successfully repay this debt, he defaulted on his loans, and what started as an unmanageable debt has become a lifelong financial albatross. Moreover, Robert is stuck at a relatively high interest rate and is locked into the lender due to the federal law that prohibits refinancing of the debt. Robert is, in a sense, a very profitable possession of the lender.

Medical Problems in the Family

A great number of borrowers were thrust into financial insolvency due to family medical situations, and many were forced into bankruptcy because of overwhelming medical bills. In these cases, student loans, being nondischargeable in bankruptcy and inescapable unless the borrower can prove total and permanent disability, become a crushing weight—particularly after the penalties and fees that result from defaulting. Ellen in Pennsylvania is a good example of this.

After her husband died in an auto accident, she was forced to sell their possessions and move back home with her parents. Ellen started looking into the possibility of going to school for some kind of training to improve her future. Soon, Ellen—a high school dropout who'd managed to earn a GED—was encouraged to go to college. She financed this by working part-time, getting some grants, and taking out federally guaranteed loans from the Pennsylvania Higher Education Assistance Agency (PHEAA), one of the country's larger nonprofit state student loan companies.

While in school, she made the dean's list and received other honors. After graduation, she went on to graduate school, again maintaining a very high grade point average. Unfortunately, her life began to go in a different direction when her father had a heart attack and then a stroke. Ellen was needed at home to help her elderly mother take care of him. She began working at a part-time job and took an economic-hardship deferment for her loans for a while, fully intending to return to graduate school. However, her father's condition worsened, and her mother started having medical problems as well. She says:

> PHEAA allows someone to care for a sick child, but not a sick parent who lives in the same home. I was told I had to start pay-ing. Unfortunately, what I could pay and what they wanted were two different things. So they sent a letter to my employer and I was let go. In the meantime, I had a dad with cancer and a bad heart to take care of, and a mom with orthopedic problems. Then I found another job...paid what I could...and had to go on family leave because the end was near for my dad. That is when I was defaulted by PHEAA—supposedly a "nonprofit" or-ganization. What a joke that is. To think that the government speaks of the importance of family values—this is certainly not the case when it comes to student loans, I have found.

Since then, Ellen has been in and out of low-paying jobs with-out benefits. She has paid what she could—about five thousand dollars, she estimates—but it has never been enough to make a dent. The loan has risen from the original $14,500 loan to over thirty-one thousand dollars.

Ellen, like all defaulted borrowers, has been harassed at home and at her various workplaces. She says she has lost numerous jobs over the company's attempts to garnish her wages. She has sold almost everything she owns and is surviving largely on her eighty-five-year-old mother's pension and Social Security. "All of my pride is gone, self-confidence went away a long time ago, and my entire life and future seems completely hopeless. Oh, yes, I wound up with a bankruptcy, but of course the loan is never excused."

Ellen has tried contacting legislators to get some kind of relief, but she has been stonewalled at every step. "I agree that something needs to be done about this, but no one listens—politicians certainly don't, and everyone else looks upon us as losers and deadbeats. My life is ruined. If only I would have worked my way through college slowly and paid for it as I went—or not gone at all. Maybe the factory work wasn't so bad after all—at least there I had my dignity."

Private Loans

Another type of consumer who is saddled with unmanageable student loan debt is the borrower who has taken out a private loan. The numbers in this group are growing very quickly. These borrowers tend to realize when they're fairly young that their financial situations have become desperate. Private student loans are nondischargeable in bankruptcy, just like federal loans, but they carry far higher interest rates. These borrowers thus find themselves with skyrocketing amounts of debt more quickly than those who have federal education debt alone, but neither group of distressed borrowers has any power to negotiate for better repayment terms or for reasonable compromises.

Elizabeth, who lives in Illinois, can attest to the overwhelming burden of private loans, and hers is a fairly common story. She received a BFA in fashion design from the International Academy of Design and Technology, in Chicago. Elizabeth qualified for some federal aid but not enough to cover the cost of tuition. Her only alternative, as explained to her by the financial aid office, was to take out private loans. According to Elizabeth, the financial aid office was "less than efficient" in explaining what she was signing on for. They never explained to her how high her interest rate would be, and they told her repeatedly that this was standard procedure, that private loans were an appropriate way to cover tuition. Elizabeth borrowed thirty-six thousand dollars in private loans and forty-three thousand in federal loans. She is on a twenty-year repayment schedule for the federal loans, paying about two hundred and fifty dollars a month. She entered repayment on these loans in February 2007.

Her private loans, however, are at an interest rate of 18.125 percent, and by August 2007 they had already accrued more than fifteen thousand dollars in interest charges alone. By the time she graduated, Elizabeth lamented, her thirty-six thousand dollars in private loans had already grown to more than fifty-four thousand. Her monthly payment on her private loans alone is $860, and her combined payments exceed $1,100. Despite the fact that Elizabeth has moved back home with her parents and is working two jobs, as a waitress and as a nanny, her student loan payments currently exceed her monthly income.

Ironically, Elizabeth was offered an entry-level position as a fashion designer in New York City but was unable to accept it because the relatively low pay and high cost of living combined with her student loan debt made it impossible. Recently, she learned that by the time she retires her student loan debt to Sallie Mae, she will have paid $141,000 on what was originally a thirty-six-thousand-dollar loan. She says she has asked for clarification of her interest charges and information on how she might negotiate a lower interest rate, but the Sallie Mae call-center staff in India give her only confused and ultimately meaningless replies.

Elizabeth is unhappy with her situation, to say the least.

No one encourages you not to go to college. Even Oprah refers to student loan debt as the only good debt. I realize now that private loans to cover tuition should be avoided at all costs. Had I known what I know now, I would not have gone back to school until I was twenty-four years old. I know that I can't expect to live at home rent-free for the next thirty years while I pay on student loans. I feel like this is a form of loan sharking, where financial aid offices and higher education institutes are pushing students into beginning a life of debt while the student is under the assumption they are bettering their quality of life by obtaining a degree, which, in this particular case, I will never be able to use. It should be illegal to prey on those that are trying to get an education.

Elizabeth takes full responsibility for the total amount that she borrowed to fund her education and has every intention of paying back what she borrowed. However, at the moment she is swimming in debt due to interest rates and capitalized interest; she hasn't been able to afford even medical insurance for more than four years. She says she has "no quality of life" and is severely depressed.

Cosigning Parents

There has been an alarming increase in the number of parents who are faced with financial ruin because they cosigned loans for their children. This is due primarily to the explosive growth of high-interest private loans in the past decade, but it is also fueled by a growing number of parents who are taking out federally guaranteed PLUS loans so their children can go to college. In both cases, bankruptcy is not an option for these loans, and parents often have to liquidate assets in order to satisfy this debt.

The Smalls are a middle-class family without sufficient resources to pay for their son, Andrew, to go to college. In 2001, Andrew was accepted to the Brooks Institute of Photography, which was a dream come true for the Smalls. He didn't receive any scholarships from this school, and the Smalls were told that the only help Andrew could get was a Stafford loan of about ten thousand dollars and private loans from Stillwater Bank that totaled ninety-five thousand dollars. The interest rates on the private loans were about 14 percent; his parents cosigned the loans.

Andrew dropped out of school after three years, just short of receiving his bachelor's degree. His mother, Beccie, says that he dropped out because he couldn't justify borrowing another forty-five thousand dollars for the last year, which he called "fluff." Andrew tried to generate enough income to pay for his living expenses and for the loans, which were $966 a month. Then the family's financial circumstances changed; the husband retired, and Beccie is now disabled with multiple sclerosis. The interest rate on the private loan is over 17 percent and rising, and they simply don't have the income to pay thirteen hundred dollars a month. The loan balance has ballooned to more than $130,000, and it is growing by more than five thousand dollars a quarter.

The Smalls are extremely concerned. "We fear for our son's future. Being saddled with what we called the uncontrollable Blob Monster will certainly ruin it. When Sallie Mae took over the loans, we were hopeful that they would have a student-friendly program for repayment. Instead we found that the loans were being run by loan sharks."

Fleeing the Country

A growing number of borrowers are admitting that they left the country exclusively because of their student loan debts. One such "student loan refugee" is Jeremy Locarno. Jeremy took out loans for both his undergraduate and law degrees. One of the reasons he went to law school was that he was having trouble paying his loans from his undergraduate education; he thought that an advanced degree would improve his financial situation. He did the homework, researching job-placement rates, average salaries, and other information about the school he eventually decided to attend. Jeremy admits that in hindsight he was quite naïve and didn't view their promotional materials with the skepticism he should have.

His grades in law school were "okay, but not great." At the end of his first year, Jeremy, like most of his classmates, was unable to find a job. He found a freelance clerking position that paid ten dollars an hour. Jeremy reflects on this lack of opportunity while in school: "The writing was clearly on the wall then and I should have cut my losses and dropped out. But I don't like to quit and still believed that education was the key to success."

Upon graduation, Jeremy was a hundred thousand dollars in debt, and the only job he could find paid forty-five thousand a year; his student loan payments represented roughly 70 percent of his monthly take-home pay. Jeremy deferred his loans for a while and looked for a better job, but without any luck. His deferments ended and his loan payments began.

He tried hard to repay his loans. In addition to practicing law, he worked as the manager of an apartment building in exchange for reduced rent. To economize, he got a roommate and drove a ten-year-old car. Nonetheless, he still couldn't manage even the interest payments on his loans. Every month the statements came and the balances were larger and larger. By 2006, his balance was more than two hundred thousand dollars, despite what he had already paid. "It was compounding so fast I could see myself owing a million dollars in a few years," he said.

The psychological stress of this debt affected Jeremy's ability to do his job.

> I honestly believe that being that much in debt really had an impact on my ability to make money. I was so worried about it. Of course, when you are under that kind of pressure, money avoids you. It's tough to get clients when you seem desperate for them. Instead of conveying confidence, I conveyed fear and anxiety. Not qualities one wants in an attorney. The psychological burden of this debt began to take a toll. It seemed that no matter how hard I worked, I would never be able to pay them off. I would never be able to get married and have children. It wasn't just the luxuries of life, fancy cars and vacations, that were beyond my reach. It was also the very things that make life worth living seemed unattainable. I used to see people with kids, and my heart would break. Lots of people raise kids on $45,000 a year. But I was making that and had loan payments that were substantially more than my monthly salary. A family just didn't seem possible.

Borrowers talk about how difficult the holidays can be. Jeremy's parents and siblings were in New York, he lived in Los Angeles, and he simply couldn't afford a ticket to see them. He recalls, "I would look at the people arriving at the homes and apartments in my neighborhood bearing gifts and know that I couldn't afford to give anybody anything. My mother had a stroke, and I didn't have the money to go see her."

Borrowers also talk about their terror of growing old and retiring. Jeremy notes, "The only thing I could live on when I retired was Social Security. And now Sallie Mae was going to take a chunk of that as well! It was even hard to make friends because I was always worried that they would say, Let's go to a movie, let's grab dinner, let's go do something. I completely isolated myself from my friends and didn't want to make new ones just because I didn't want to have to be in the position of spending ten bucks for a movie. In retrospect it seems ridiculous, but that was how paranoid I was about trying to pay these loans. Meanwhile Sallie Mae was calling me, calling my family, calling friends I hadn't seen in years and harassing them."

At one point, Jeremy says he was "so drunk and depressed that I tied a plastic bag around my head and lay down in bed hoping to never wake up. The only thing that saved me was a conversation I had had with my sister about a month earlier when I told her I was suicidal. She had the rote response about how terrible that would be but then she added, 'Think of my kids. That would be part of their history, part of their lives, something they would have to live with forever.' I just couldn't do that. I ripped the bag off my head. Now it just seems ridiculous to have wanted to even try."

Like many student loan borrowers whose debt exploded beyond manageability, Jeremy had had enough. A friend who was living in Asia suggested that Jeremy visit him, and the friend even paid for the trip. He told Jeremy it was for some legal consulting, but Jeremy says it was pretty obvious the friend was trying to help him out and was suggesting that Jeremy simply leave the country. Jeremy did indeed visit his friend and did indeed move. He now works as an English teacher and is relatively happy. "I'm able to save money, go out with friends, do some traveling. I'm not living like a wealthy man. But I am a thousand times happier than I was before. I am much more optimistic about my future."

Jeremy believes that he should have been able to file for bankruptcy, as people routinely do with other types of debt. "I made a mistake in going to law school and taking out loans to pay for it. But I truly believed that education was the key to success. Donald Trump made a mistake when he overextended to build his empire a few years back. He declared bankruptcy and started with a clean slate. All of the airline companies have declared bankruptcy a number of times. Only student loans are not dischargeable in bankruptcy, so this option was not available to me. Make a mistake with Sallie Mae and you will live with it for the rest of your life."

Senior Citizens Losing Social Security Benefits

One increasingly common tactic used by guarantors and collection companies to extract wealth from student loan debtors is Social Security garnishment. Typically, this is an administrative action; in other words, in the case of defaulted student loans, no court order is required to attach a senior citizen's benefits. Federal disability income can also be garnished in this manner.

After her husband passed away, fifty-six-year-old Lorraine Hughes of California went back to college, and she took out a fifteen-hundred-dollar loan to do so. But her oldest son was killed, and she was forced to withdraw from school and move to a different part of the state to help settle his affairs. She says she contacted the lender to explain that she was surviving on a small widow's pension and was assured that the loan would be forgiven.

About five years later, Lorraine applied for a regular loan and was turned down. She immediately contacted the credit bureau and learned that several student loans in her name were in default. She contacted the lender, who agreed that the amount was wrong—she had borrowed about fifteen hundred dollars but they were showing that she owed four thousand. The lender told her that that there was no way the loan would have been forgiven, even under the dire circumstances in which she had found herself. Lorraine explained that she was living on a small Social Security check and couldn't pay the loan, and she didn't hear from the lender again until March 2006, when the company attached her Social Security check. Her Social Security income was $786 per month, and thirty-six dollars a month was taken from it. The collection company now claims that she owes more than twelve thousand dollars on the original loan. Lorraine is seventy-four years old, and Social Security is her only income.

Student Loan Suicides

Tragically, a growing number of people whose family members have committed suicide as a result of student loan debt are coming forward.

In September 2007, Jason Yoder, a thirty-five-year-old recent graduate of Illinois State University, was found dead in a chemistry lab on campus—the same chemistry lab where he had done the research to complete his master's thesis. He had complained to relatives that he was feeling "lower than low," could not find a job, and that his student loans had grown to a hundred thousand dollars.

As his mother was preparing for his funeral, she was harassed by collection calls from individuals wanting to know when he would pay up.[1]

Michele Guidoni also received his master's degree in chemistry. According to his mother, Gail, Michele was severely depressed because his student loans had grown to more than two hundred thousand dollars; he had consolidated them at a high interest rate and was unable to refinance the debt when the rates dropped. This hard-line rule became overwhelming for Michele, and on September 28, 2005, he shot and killed himself.

Gail Guidoni feels that her son's loss was particularly tragic for the family. "The world lost a beautiful, brilliant person and I lost one of the loves of my life. I'm not just saying these things because I am his mother and I loved him. He was so smart he belonged to Mensa." Gail says she still receives bills from the student loan company, even though she has repeatedly returned them to the sender with the message that he is deceased. In Gail Guidoni's view, Michele's suicide had many victims, including herself, Michele's wife, and his father.

An unsigned submission was received at StudentLoanJus tice.org in March 2006 from someone in Maryland whose sister had committed suicide. Because of the anonymity of this submission and the impossibility of vetting the source, it is posted here in its entirety for the reader's examination:

> I am writing to tell my sister's story. She is no longer with us . . . She took her life a year ago. My sister was the first in our family to attend college. She graduated from Johns Hopkins University and did really well for a while. In her early thirties, she became ill (breast cancer) and was unable to work. I am not sure how she was paying her loans, but I know the student loan representatives were hounding her. I spoke with several on her behalf and little if anything was ever accomplished.
>
> My sister was out of work for a very long time, as chemo made her very ill. She was repeatedly called by student loan representatives even when told how ill she was. I do not want to go into a great deal of detail, but I will say that my sister took her life because she said she simply did not want to live anymore. What is interesting is that my sister was not terminally ill. Her cancer was in stage two . . . and her prognosis was very good. What ultimately led to my sister's death is the way she was repeatedly hounded by collection agencies regarding her student loans. I wrote to a Maryland senator myself and stated that something has to be done about this. People are being penalized for going after their dreams of becoming educated. Does anyone else see something wrong with this picture?
>
> My sister's life has been an inspiration to me. I have decided to go back to school. I promised her that I would not obtain any student loans . . . I am doing it the old-fashioned way. . . . I am working three jobs to finance my education. I will be somewhere in my early forties when I finish, but at least I won't be literally worried to death over student loans.

CHAPTER FIVE

The Oversight Fiasco

Since the mid-1990s, there has been frequent and consistent criticism of the U.S. Department of Education's oversight of student loan companies. This criticism has come from a variety of sources, including members of Congress, public interest groups, and grassroots organizations. Even the Office of the Inspector General for the U.S. Department of Education has issued scathing criticisms regarding the department's oversight of its loan programs.

Two crucial developments occurred at the U.S. Department of Education during the 1990s. First, the department's higher education offices were virtually taken over from within when former Sallie Mae executives, as well as executives of other student loan companies, were given key management positions there.[1] Second, during this time, the Direct Loan Program, which bypassed the banks in the lending process, was systematically weakened. These events laid the groundwork for inappropriate and even illegal activities that ultimately benefited the lenders and Department of Education employees at the expense of the students and taxpayers.

The potential for conflict of interest within the department was noted in a fall 2006 report issued by the Office of the Inspector General.[2] Shortly thereafter, in 2006 and 2007, it was discovered that not only had department officials allowed the federal government to be massively overbilled by lenders, but a key official (a former Sallie Mae employee) had held stock in one of the lending companies he was overseeing. Also, the U.S. Department of Education farmed out many of its oversight functions to state guaranty agencies and even to lending companies such as Sallie Mae, organizations that often abused their powers for the sake of increased revenue; the department colluded with those companies that they were supposed to be overseeing. In the wake of these and other discoveries made by the media, the U.S. Senate, and the New York attorney general, Secretary of Education Margaret Spellings conceded before Congress in a May 2007 hearing that the system was "redundant, Byzantine, and broken."[3] Shortly thereafter, multiple staff members, including the head of the Office of Federal Student Aid, left the department.

While the depth and breadth of such conflicts of interest among the U.S. Department of Education, guaranty agencies, and lenders are not currently known, disturbing examples that have surfaced—thanks to dogged investigation by student advocates, members of the free press, and former U.S. Department of Education employees—are detailed in this chapter.

Assault on the Direct Loan Program

With the presidential election of 2000, dramatic changes began to happen within the U.S. Department of Education. President Bush appointed William Hansen, former president of the Education Finance Council (a consortium of FFEL lenders), to the number-two position in the department. In the past, Hansen had made negative remarks about the Direct Loan Program to Congress; now he was in charge of it. In 2002, a proposal was made to sell off the Direct Loan Program's loan portfolio to a private company. Hansen denied claims that this was an attempt to kill the program,[4] but other activities that followed made the

Bush administration's intentions concerning the Direct Loan Program quite clear.

In 2002, President Bush appointed Theresa Shaw to head the Office of Federal Student Aid. Prior to joining the U.S. Department of Education, Shaw had been a vice president at Sallie Mae. When Shaw began working at the department, she brought with her a group of individuals from Sallie Mae, none of whom had had experience in the public sector. Given these developments, it was apparent that the Department of Education, the Bush administration, and Congress were, in effect, trying to kill the Direct Loan Program. According to Barmak Nassirian of the American Association of Collegiate Registrars and Admissions Officers, "The [Bush] administration is causing a slow strangulation of the Direct Loan Program."[5] There were also strong advocates for the elimination of the Direct Loan Program from powerful Republican congressmen, including Buck McKeon and John Boehner. Congressman Pete Hoekstra (R-MI) issued a blunt statement about the Direct Loan Program: "We should put a stake through its heart."[6]

Attempts were made to move the Direct Loan funding into a discretionary account, which would be easier for Congress to redirect; it was owing to public congressional actions only that this was not completed. Clearly, in the absence of outside action, the U.S. Department of Education would turn the Direct Loan Program into a relic.

There were efforts by certain Democrats and a few Republican members of Congress to save the Direct Loan Program, but the multipronged assault on it by Sallie Mae, the Consumer Bankers Association, and other student loan interests established an almost overwhelming force against direct lending. Congress also participated in weakening the program, making it more difficult to consolidate into DL. This was largely a fight between the Democrats, who were led by Senator Kennedy, and the Republicans. Indeed, the Direct Loan Program's market share dwindled from its high mark of 34 percent in 1997 to about 19 percent by 2007.[7]

The weakening of the Direct Loan Program was a testament to the strength of the Sallie Mae lobbying presence on Capitol Hill, as well as to its growing influence within the U.S. Department of Education. Three separate reports concluded that the Direct Loan Program was cheaper for the taxpayers than other programs[8]—even the Bush administration (which has close ties to the student loan industry) conceded in its fiscal year 2005 budget request that the Federal Family Education Loan (FFEL) Program cost the taxpayers eleven dollars more for every hundred dollars lent than the Direct Loan Program did.[9] This evidence of the lower cost of the Direct Loan Program won support for it from some fiscally conservative Republicans, including Rep. Thomas Petri (R-WI), but those voices were drowned out by Republican colleagues who apparently had other motives for their championing of the FFEL Program over the Direct Loan Program.

The Inspector General's Warning

In September 2006, the Office of the Inspector General issued a report to Theresa Shaw, head of the Federal Student Aid Office, following its inspection of the Financial Partners division, the U.S. Department of Education office that oversaw the privately administered federal loan program. OIG found that Financial Partners did not provide even *adequate* oversight and also did not consistently enforce program requirements.[10] The report noted that the office emphasized partnership over compliance in its mission statements, and that it did not adequately review, test, identify, or report instances of noncompliance.[11] It was also pointed out that the turnover rate of the managerial positions for Financial Partners was too high. However, in light of evidence that surfaced soon after, the turnover continued.

The Federal Student Aid Office did not take kindly to the criticism. According to the Office of the Inspector General, FSA often made statements and conclusions that disputed the findings of the report, but it did not give reasons for the disagreements, nor did it provide the data necessary to support its position, even when the OIG requested it.[12]

The OIG report concluded that the collective deficiencies found in Financial Partners' management philosophy, policies, procedures, and operations created a weak environment for monitoring and oversight of the FFEL Program.[13]

The 9.5 Percent Overbilling Scandal

The Office of the Inspector General's statements proved to be prescient indeed. In the very same month that this report was issued, the OIG discovered that the U.S. Department of Education had been inappropriately paying hundreds of millions in subsidies to Nelnet, a student loan company based in Lincoln, Nebraska.[14] This complicated scheme involved a provision in the Higher Education Act that guaranteed lenders a 9.5 percent rate of return for loans funded through nonprofit bonds that had been issued prior to 1993. Initially, this provision was a response to the high interest rate environment of the 1980s, and these loans were supposed to be canceled by the department after a certain time. However, certain lenders attempted to keep these loans alive and in fact actually *grew* them through inappropriate accounting methods.

Nelnet, for example, had implemented a plan called Project 950. Under this plan, the company transferred loans into and out of tax-exempt obligations from taxable obligations through a process called recycling or cloning, and the company continued to bill under the 9.5 percent plan. In this manner, they could effectively transform a great number of loans into 9.5 percent loans—far more profitable than standard FFEL loans of the time. Nelnet thus effectively increased the amount of loans qualifying for this increased subsidy, going from approximately $551 million in March 2003 to roughly $3.66 billion in June 2004. It was estimated in the report that through this dubious accounting method, Nelnet overbilled the federal government by about $278 million.[15]

Nelnet was not the only lending company using this recycling process in order to bill the U.S. Department of Education for higher subsidies; many others were implicated as well. It was only through the actions of Jon Oberg, a department employee who's now retired, that these overbillings came to light. "I have come across what appears to be significant federal waste," department researcher Jon H. Oberg wrote in a 2003 memo to agency officials. "I estimate it amounts to about $30,000 per day, perhaps more."[16]

According to an analysis performed by Mr. Oberg, between 2003 and 2006, the Department of Education paid out a total of $716 million in claims to ten FFEL lenders, and most of that money—some $400 million—went to Nelnet. Between 1993 and 2001, subsidy payments on these sunsetted loans totaled about $1.1 billion.[17] The *Washington Post* performed an independent analysis in October 2007 and found that between 2003 and 2006, overpayments to Nelnet amounted to at least $278 million and that illegal overpayments to other lenders during the same period could have been as much as $330 million.[18] According to a staff member at a New Hampshire lender that had returned money after discovering this error, "It seemed like they would pay subsidies to almost anyone without checking at all."[19]

Oberg and other analysts had attempted to convince department officials to address this issue but had been largely unsuccessful. A July 2004 e-mail reporting this problem to appropriate management personnel within the department disclosed what amounted to billions in improper payments. It was noted at the end of the e-mail, which was sent by Mirek Halaska, that the department would "get kicked hard for this issue sometime down the road."[20]

In 2004, Senator Kennedy called for legislation to require the U.S. Department of Education to recoup these funds from the lenders.[21] Unfortunately, the Republican Congress did not do so. "A year ago, Senate Democrats proposed legislation to shut both loopholes down once and for all. The Senate Republicans did not act on that proposal, did not introduce their own legislation, and did not hold a single hearing. They asked no oversight questions of the Bush administration. In short, they did nothing."[22]

Shockingly, these improper-payment claims were initially forgiven by management at the U.S. Department of Education, which decided not to pursue repayment. Secretary Spellings commented that the department bore some responsibility for the confusion over these payments, and Diane Jones, the assistant secretary, asserted that meaningful inferences couldn't be made from the department data.[23] Jon Oberg found this assertion incredible. "I find it strange that four experts (cited in the *Post*) can quickly verify estimates of illegal claims, but the department says no one can possibly know—and apparently they don't care," he stated in an October 2007 conversation.

It is important to note that the managers of Financial Partners from 2002 to 2007 were brought in from the same lending interests that the office was in charge of overseeing. Kristie Hansen, manager of the office from 2002 to 2005, came to Financial Partners from the National Council of Higher Education Loan Programs (NCHELP), and her chief of staff, Tim Cameron, had been her colleague at NCHELP before joining her to run the office. When she was selected to head the Financial Partners division, Education Undersecretary William Hansen remarked that he was delighted that the department was able to attract such an "experienced partner from the community of student loan providers."[24]

The 9.5 percent scandal provided a glimpse of the inner workings of the U.S. Department of Education and, in particular, of how deeply that office was stacked with industry insiders. In a 2007 exchange regarding the 2004 e-mail that first brought this issue to light, Mr. Oberg noted:

> The first three recipients of that e-mail were industry people brought in to ED: Sutphin, Fontana, and O'Brien, all of whom were Sallie Mae people. The Financial Partners office was headed in those years by Kristie Hansen and her chief of staff, Tim Cameron, both brought in from NCHELP. Of course Terry Shaw from Sallie Mae and Sally Stroup from PHEAA were in charge of FSA and OPE, respectively. Kathleen Smith (of PHEAA and EFC) was in John Boehner's office, supervising from the Hill.

In January 2008, the U.S. Department of Education ignored findings by its own Office of the Inspector General and in effect gave one lender permission to decide for itself how much of the overbilled amount, if any, it should repay. The OIG had estimated that overpayments to the Pennsylvania Higher Education Assistance Authority (PHEAA) totaled about thirty-four million dollars. However, in January of 2008, Patricia Trubia, head of Financial Partners at the department, sent a letter to PHEAA stating that the Department of Education's own estimates showed overpayments of about fifteen million dollars—far less than the OIG estimate—and further asking PHEAA to calculate for itself an estimate of what the student loan agency thought it had overpaid.[25] Keith New, spokesman for the company, said that the company might well end up with zero liability depending on the outcome of their analysis.[26]

Across the board, members of the grassroots borrower community were not impressed with this move by the department. In particular, they were not happy with Patricia Trubia, who had come to head Financial Partners under a dark cloud (discussed below) after previously running the Default Management office for the department. The fact that an individual had gone from running an office that greatly harmed borrowers through the default collection process to heading another office that effectively forgave lenders hundreds of millions of dollars in illegal billings was seen as ironic to many but fitting to many more, especially those in the StudentLoanJustice.org community.

The Fox Guarding the Henhouse: Matteo Fontana

One of the Sallie Mae executives brought into the Department of Education by Theresa Shaw—and a recipient of the 2004 e-mail detailing the 9.5 percent overbilling scandal—was Matteo Fontana. In spring of 2007, the New America Foundation discovered that Fontana had held at least a hundred thousand dollars in stock from a student loan company, Student Loan Xpress, while he was employed at the U.S. Department of Education.

The case of Fontana is significant. This was not an incident where an obscure, midlevel employee engaged in shady personal activities for financial gain. Rather, Fontana was promoted to *manage* Financial Partners, the very office charged with oversight of student lenders participating in the FFEL Program. What is perhaps worse is that other department officials were aware of his stock holdings.[27] This case caused some concern among democratic members of Congress, including Senator Ted Kennedy (D-MA), who commented, "The financial disclosure forms filed by Education Department official Matteo Fontana during his time at the department raise grave concerns about the effectiveness and impartiality of the ethics process at the department. Any American can tell you that this is dead wrong."[28]

Before he led the Financial Partners office, Fontana was in charge of the National Student Loan Data System (NSLDS). This system, which held detailed information about student borrowers, had been abused badly by some lenders, who used the information in NSLDS to market consolidation loans to students. In fact, the abuse of the NSLDS was significant enough to prompt a memo from the Office of the Inspector General to Theresa Shaw, head of the FSA, demanding that her office limit lenders' access to the database.[29] Given the clear abuse that occurred on Fontana's watch at the NSLDS, it seems unlikely that anyone would promote him to head the office of Financial Partners, but in fact, that is what Ms. Shaw did, effectively putting the fox in charge of the henhouse.

In May of 2006, when this news story broke, Secretary Margaret Spellings placed Fontana on administrative leave and promised an investigation into the stock holdings of other U.S. Department of Education employees. As of February 2008, the department had not yet made the results of this investigation public.

Systemic Oversight Problems with the Student Loan Program

While these recent oversight scandals within the U.S. Department of Education are both dramatic and alarming, there are deeper systemic problems that are even more crucial and disturbing. These involve collusive relationships between the companies who make student loans and their guarantors, those entities legally designated to oversee the lenders' operations.

Guarantors ensure that lenders comply with the law when they collect and administer federally guaranteed student loans. This means ascertaining that diligent efforts are being made by the lenders to collect loan payments and supervising other activities that protect against students' default. In the event that a student does default on his or her loans, the guarantors are required by law to take over, or purchase, the loans and then pay the lender the value of the loans at the time of default, which includes principal and accrued interest. The guarantors can then employ the powers granted to them by Congress to collect on these loans from the students.

In practice, however, the student loan system has deteriorated to the point that guarantors derive a significant portion of their income from defaulted loans and so have been known to engage in collusive relationships with the lenders they oversee, allowing the lenders facilitate student default, which thereby increases the guarantors' revenue. Even worse: since the mid-1990s, lenders such as Sallie Mae have actually been acquiring the assets of the guarantors who are supposed to be overseeing them.

Collusive Relationships

In 2007, in the midst of the various scandals surfacing in the student loan industry, a reporter for the *Newark Star-Ledger*, Ana Alaya, found that the New Jersey Higher Education Student Assistance Authority (HESAA) had engaged in a contract with Sallie Mae. The agreement was that HESAA would steer state schools to use Sallie Mae as a preferred lender and in return would receive cash payments based on the amount of loans that those schools' students borrowed from Sallie Mae.

Over a seven-year period, HESAA received a $2.2 million payment on an annual basis—a total of more than $15 million, for promoting Sallie Mae, informing students of Sallie Mae's benefits, coordinating and processing guarantees for loans originated through Sallie Mae, integrating loan-delivery systems with Sallie Mae, and offering technical assistance to institutions for these loans.[30]

This agreement benefited Sallie Mae tremendously. As of 2007, Sallie Mae was easily the largest lender for at least a half a dozen universities and colleges across the state. While the director of HESAA denied that the agency steered students toward any particular lender, at least one university representative confirmed that this was the case. Dave Muha, a spokesman for

Drew University, stated that the university decided to exclusively market Sallie Mae loans to students. "We did that at the encouragement of HESAA and we did that because there's a streamlined processing of loans and promise of service," he said in an April interview. He continued, "From our perspective, there really is no reason to question a state agency set up to serve the interests of students going to school in the state." Muha noted that the university was unaware that HESAA was receiving payments from Sallie Mae in return for loan volume.[31]

Upon this discovery, HESAA immediately terminated its agreement with Sallie Mae, as well as a similar agreement the agency had struck with Nelnet, another notorious lender in the industry.

Conflicts of Interest by Acquisition

As Sallie Mae grew to dominate the student lending industry, it counted among its acquisitions a number of entities related to state loan guarantors, including assets of the Northwest Education Loan Association (NELA) and, most notably, the USA Group, acquired in 2000. The USA Group was an umbrella organization for a state guarantor, USA Funds, and it included a number of for-profit and nonprofit entities in a highly complicated network. These companies together originated loans, serviced them, and collected on defaulted accounts, performing almost the entire range of functions involved in the administration of student loans.

Sallie Mae bought all the elements of this organization that it could, which included nearly everything but the nonprofit guarantor agency, which it was not legally allowed to buy. The details of the USA Group acquisition by Sallie Mae are given in chapter 2, but it essentially involved a fifty-million-dollar payout to the board members who approved the sale.

Regardless of the board members' financial motivations, a dangerous precedent was set when a lender acquired the assets of a guarantor, an organization whose function was overseeing the student lenders. The groundwork was laid for conflicts of interest to occur. With this acquisition, Sallie Mae could not only originate and service loans but also oversee the collections of defaulted loans—a more profitable arrangement than letting an outside collection company do the job. Technically, Sallie Mae was not guaranteeing the loans—this function resided with the nonprofit guarantor agency—but its newly acquired subsidiary had a service contract with the guarantor that paid Sallie Mae some $250 million a year.[32] Today, USA Funds is a "shell of its former self," with only seventy-five employees; the Sallie Mae staff carries out the majority of its functions. In effect, Sallie Mae found a way to gain oversight authority over itself.[33]

Senator Ted Kennedy and Congressman George Miller, chairmen, respectively, of the Senate and House Education committees, voiced concerns about these arrangements. Even U.S. Department of Education regulators shared this concern. An April 2002 audit by the U.S. Department of Education's inspector general concluded that Sallie Mae's relationship with USA Funds represented a legal violation because of the fact that the USA Group (wholly owned by Sallie Mae) was providing staff to USA Funds.

However, the Department of Education gave Sallie Mae a pass for these activities. On December 28, 2004, Matteo Fontana issued a ruling defying the inspector general's audit. In the letter, Fontana declared that Sallie Mae could legally perform debt-collection services for a partner company, USA Funds, even though federal conflict-of-interest regulations prohibited such work by the same entity that held the loan.[34]

It should be noted that USA Funds was no stranger to allegations of wrongdoing. In fact, it had a long history of highly suspicious activities. In 1996, Senator Paul Simon (D-IL) and his staff (which included Robert Shireman) had become deeply alarmed that a nonprofit guarantor agency was earning revenue by engaging in activities well outside the IRS limits for charitable activities.[35] Simon and his staff found that USA Funds had vastly underreported their lobbying activities and that their staff salaries were exorbitant by any standards, which took away from the needy students they claimed to serve. Simon voiced strong concerns about an overcharging scheme in which an affiliate of the company was overcharging the nonprofit, thus taking away funds from its tax-exempt purpose. As a result of these and other concerns about the company, Senator Simon had called for an IRS investigation. In the letter to the IRS, Simon concluded, "It is clear from the information I have reviewed that the USA Group is either violating any number of tax laws or is certainly pushing the envelope to its extreme limits."[36]

Since the scandals of spring 2007, Fontana has been placed on administrative leave and Theresa Shaw has resigned from her position in the Department of Education. Shaw announced her resignation shortly after the Fontana scandal broke. Fontana was suspended and has since been under investigation. It is interesting to note, however, that both realized significant monetary benefits from their employment at the Department of Education, despite these very serious revelations. As of January 2008, Fontana was still on paid leave with the department. Shaw, for all the scandals that came to light during her time with the department, was awarded bonuses totaling $250,000 between 2003 and 2006, in addition to her salary.

More frustrating, however, is the fact that the systemic problems that existed during their tenures persist today. The Department of Education, instead of performing the role that it is required by law to perform—overseeing both the FFELP and Direct Loan Program—displays a maddening resistance to acknowledge and correct the systemic oversight failures that have been brought to light and continues to act in the best interests of FFEL lenders, at the expense of borrowers and taxpayers.

CHAPTER SIX

The Corruption of the Universities

As the burden of paying for college was shifted to students and the cost of college tuition exploded, lending agencies, guarantors, and collection companies were not the only entities maneuvering to capitalize on this new source of wealth—colleges and universities were also caught up in the fray. By 2000, it became apparent that some schools had all but abandoned even the pretense of concern for students' financial well-being and were entering into agreements with lenders for the purpose of making additional money from students, over and above the loan income that was being paid to them for the cost of attendance.

As a general rule, students are highly vulnerable to exploitation in this area. By the time they set foot on campus, they are already on the hook. With unbridled optimism about their futures and innate trust of their universities, students tend to sign nearly anything their universities put in front of them in order to get registered for class. After all, they have already made the decision to attend college, typically years before they get there. They have already gone through the difficult task of applying for and gaining acceptance to the universities. By the time a student must decide from whom to borrow money, or whether to borrow money at all, the groundwork has been laid, and the student will almost certainly accept any recommendations the school gives. Most former students cannot even recall actually making a choice of lenders while they were in college.

This is the reason that it is so important for the universities and their financial aid offices to look out for the best financial interests of the students. Violations of the trust that exists between the universities and their students could have devastating financial consequences down the road and should be taken extremely seriously.

Investigations by the New York State attorney general Eliot Spitzer and his successor, Andrew Cuomo, the U.S. Senate, the public, and the media uncovered a broad and deep assortment of illegal and unethical activities by higher education institutions and lenders. These ranged from the sublime to the obscene and were found across the academic spectrum, from Ivy League universities, such as Columbia and the University of Pennsylvania, to top-tier universities, including the University of Southern California and the University of Texas at Austin, to obscure trade schools.

As shocking as these discoveries were (many were reported on the front pages of major newspapers), the most important truth that these scandals revealed was that the higher education system had become beholden to the lenders. Their interests had become aligned to the point that they were a political force, an "unholy alliance" between lenders and universities (as Attorney General Cuomo characterized it), and they had trampled on the very students they claimed to serve.

Institutional Kickbacks
One would hope that an unsavory term like *kickback* wouldn't be used in the context of higher education; it conjures up the image of corrupt elected officials, organized crime, and the like. In 2007, however, this word was used by respected officials, noted

news organizations, and others to describe what was happening in academia with respect to student loans.

It had been well known for years that universities were entering into discreet agreements with lenders in which the schools were paid by the lenders over and above what they were already receiving in tuition. In May 2006, *60 Minutes* aired a segment on student loans, and this phenomenon entered into the public consciousness. In this segment, Michael Dannenberg, director of education policy at the New America Foundation, called these arrangements what they were: kickbacks.[1]

The scheme Dannenberg was referring to, known as the school-as-lender program, is fairly simple: the university makes loans directly to students, then a lender repurchases the loans from the school at a premium in addition to paying the university "administrative fees." In return, the university agrees to promote this lender's loans exclusively.

Eliot Spitzer's Investigation

Following the *60 Minutes* report, multiple groups, including Stu dentLoanJustice.org members and lending companies who had been shut out of the business, appealed to the New York State attorney general's office to investigate these suspect practices. One lender, called My Rich Uncle, even took out a full-page ad in the *New York Times* to complain about arrangements it referred to as kickbacks and payola. The result was a wide-ranging investigation spearheaded by Spitzer. After Spitzer became governor of New York, the investigation was continued by his successor, Andrew Cuomo (son of Mario Cuomo). On March 15, 2007, initial findings of the investigation were made public. Attorney General Cuomo noted that the "unholy alliance" of lenders and institutions of higher learning had taken hold and was not serving the interests of the students. Specifically, the investigation found that:

- Lenders were paying kickbacks to universities based on a percentage of loan volume that the school's financial aid offices steered toward the lenders.
- Lenders gave all-expenses-paid trips to financial aid administrators and their families to exotic destinations, including Pebble Beach, California, and the Caribbean. They also provided colleges with computer systems and put financial aid administrators into paid positions on their advisory boards.
- Lenders set up funds and credit lines for schools to use, in exchange for those schools putting the lenders on their preferred-lender lists.
- Lenders offered large sums of money to universities to drop out of the government's Direct Loan Program.
- Lenders ran call centers on behalf of universities, often answering phones claiming to be representatives of the universities' financial aid offices when in fact they were employees of lending companies.
- Lenders on preferred-lender lists had agreements to sell their loans to a single lender, thus eliminating any real choice for the students.
- Sales of loans often wiped out the back-end benefits promised to students without the students ever knowing. This includes interest reduction for on-time payments, reductions for electronic payments, and other benefits.[2]

The New York investigation sent shock waves across the higher education landscape. A month after this investigation became public, six universities that had been targeted by the investigation—the University of Pennsylvania, New York University, Syracuse, Fordham, Long Island University, and St. Johns —agreed to reimburse former students a total of $3.27 million for inflated loans. By July 2007, ten major lenders had each agreed to pay between five hundred thousand and two million dollars into a national education fund established by Cuomo.[3]

Despite the colleges' and lenders' quick acknowledgments of wrongdoing, standard consumer protections remain as unavailable for college students today as they were prior to the investigation. Attorney General Cuomo realized this and commented that it would be appropriate to revisit bankruptcy laws with respect to student loans, suggesting that the federal government should look out for the interests of the students as aggressively as it had fought for the interests of the lenders.[4]

The U.S. Senate Investigation

In June and September 2007, the U.S. Senate Committee on Health, Education, Labor, and Pensions (HELP) released reports on its own investigation into marketing practices by FFEL lenders. These reports confirmed what the New York investigation had uncovered, as well as much more. The reports clearly showed that not only were student loan companies providing compensation to universities in the expectation that they would secure positions on the schools' preferred-lender lists, they were also paying financial aid administrators directly—and some administrators actually held stock in the same lending companies that were on their colleges' preferred-lender lists.

The reports, which made use of internal e-mails, provided compelling evidence that university officials viewed their preferred-lender lists as bargaining chips, using them not only to secure payments for the universities but also to reap their own personal benefits. Some officials played lenders against one another, and there was evidence of various schemes designed to benefit the administrators or the school rather than to assist students. The following includes specific cases that the Senate reports focused on.

The University of Texas at Austin: Larry Loves Tequila

The Senate investigation found that the University of Texas at Austin's financial aid office, which was headed by Dr. Lawrence

Burt, made decisions regarding lender inclusion on its preferred-lender list based on treats given to Dr. Burt. An e-mail provided by a former Bank of America employee to the Senate HELP Committee detailed a meeting with Mr. Don Davis, associate director of student financial services at the University of Texas at Austin; it was noted that Dr. Burt had certain expectations from lenders that were at the top of the preferred-lender lists.

The e-mail stated that the top lenders provided staff with annual luncheons, happy hours, "parties for Larry's family," all-expenses-paid invitations to golf tournaments, and tickets to sporting events. It further stated that Dr. Burt "loves tequila and wine" and that he had not had to purchase these spirits since becoming director at the university.[5]

At one point in the meeting with Don Davis, this Bank of America employee had expressed confusion, saying that he didn't understand how a lender fulfilling the list of expectations given would grow its business by 20 to 30 percent. According to the e-mail: "Don's response to me—some things I am not allowed to share." When questioned about this e-mail transcript of the meeting, Mr. Davis could not recall what was meant by this.

Dr. Burt served on the advisory boards of many lending institutions, including Citibank, Sallie Mae, the Access Group, A+ Med Funds, CLC, Chase, Loan Star Lenders, Student Loan Xpress, University Federal Credit Union, and Wells Fargo. How he came to join Citibank's advisory board was investigated in further detail by the Senate: Documents examined during the investigation showed that Dr. Burt demanded favors that Citibank deemed inappropriate; because Citibank did not perform these favors, Dr. Burt dropped the company from the undergraduate preferred-lender list for the 2005–2006 academic year. According to the Senate report, Citibank tried to regain its position on the list by inviting Dr. Burt to serve on its advisory board, providing expensive entertainment and donating to charities of Dr. Burt's choosing; these favors were rewarded by Dr. Burt's restoring Citibank to the preferred-lender list the following year.

Johns Hopkins University

The 2007 Senate reports also examined Johns Hopkins University and found a similar pattern of illegal payments to university officials. In the Johns Hopkins situation, the person of interest was Dr. Ellen Frishberg, financial aid director of the College of Arts and Sciences and Engineering. The Senate found that Dr. Frishberg had received payments from consulting contracts with both American Express and Student Loan Xpress. During the time period that Dr. Frishberg was being paid by these lenders, their names appeared on the preferred-lender lists at the university—lists for which she had ultimate responsibility.[6]

Dr. Frishberg was paid more than ninety-three thousand dollars by these lenders, and between 2002 and 2004, she even had twenty-one thousand dollars of her own tuition paid by Student Loan Xpress when she enrolled in the University of Pennsylvania's executive doctorate Program. Dr. Frishberg acknowledged during interviews that her colleagues were unaware that she had consulting contracts with these preferred lenders.

The report noted that Dr. Frishberg had received payments totaling forty-two thousand dollars from Collegiate Funding Services, a student loan company owned by JPMorgan Chase, and that, as was also the case with Student Loan Xpress, Dr. Frishberg did not have a written agreement with the lender— a very curious fact, especially given the large dollar amounts involved.

The University of Nebraska

In 2004, the University of Nebraska Board of Regents approved an exclusive school-as-lender arrangement with the National Education Loan Network (Nelnet) to provide loans to its students. As with other school-as-lender arrangements, this relationship brought hundreds of thousands of dollars into the university. This is disturbing, but what is more disturbing is a fact uncovered by a student reporter in February 2007: the university's nonprofit foundation owned more than eight hundred thousand shares in the lender's stock and stood to benefit greatly by the stock's appreciation.[7]

The University of Nebraska's relationship with Nelnet is yet another example of how university entanglements with lenders can cause conflicts of interest and raise huge red flags regarding the university's responsibility to the financial interests of the students. As a part of the agreement with Nelnet, the University of Nebraska dropped out of the Direct Loan Program.

Nelnet, which owns the student loan collection company in Indianapolis that houses a four-thousand-gallon shark tank in its lobby, is the focus of both Attorney General Cuomo's investigation and an ongoing investigation by the Senate regarding collection abuses. One wonders how many University of Nebraska students will be pursued by Nelnet and forced to repay far more than they originally borrowed as a direct result of being steered toward this lender by their university.

The Student Loan Xpress Stock Scandal

On April 4, 2007, the New America Foundation revealed that multiple university financial aid officials held stock in a particular student loan company. The offending officials included Dr. Burt; Catherine Thomas, director of financial aid at the University of Southern California; and David Charlow, financial aid director at Columbia University.[8] In addition, three officials had received payments from the same student loan company. These included Dr. Ellen Frishberg of Johns Hopkins University; Timothy Lehmann, financial aid director at Capella University; and Walter Cathie, assistant vice president for finance at Widener University.

Matteo Fontana, manager of the Department of Education's Financial Partners division—an office responsible for oversight of lenders—was also found to have held stock in this company while he was serving in an oversight position there (see chapter 3 for details).

The offending company was Student Loan Xpress, a subsidiary of the Education Lending Group. Student Loan Xpress was on the preferred-lender list for all of these universities, and its stock was offered to these individuals in return for service on the company's advisory board. All six of these officials were fired, resigned, or otherwise left the universities shortly after the facts became publicly known.

Blurring the Lines

In many cases, it had become impossible to tell where the universities ended and the student loan companies began. Lenders staffed call centers on behalf of universities, pretending to be unbiased employees of the university when they were actually agents of student loan companies. Running call centers was a widely used tool; Sallie Mae operated twenty such centers, and Nelnet operated seven. These arrangements were often accompanied by highly suspicious donations by the lenders to the universities.

One clear example is the case of Eastern Michigan University. Eastern Michigan agreed to let Sallie Mae employees operate a call center on its behalf, answering student questions about financial aid. At the same time, the university received about $310,000 in donations from Sallie Mae, and it also listed the company as a preferred lender.

In August 2007, as a result of the New York investigation, the university decided to return the unused portion of the Sallie Mae funds, about $161,000, in order to avoid the appearance of a conflict of interest. Officials for the university said that it would likely sever its ties with Sallie Mae for its call-center operations.[9]

Another widespread trend across the country is that universities allow lenders to perform loan counseling for students. This practice is seen by critics as nothing more than marketing opportunities for lenders. In fact, it is well known that when loan representatives are offering exit counseling to students, they frequently steer students toward consolidating their loans with whichever lenders the loan representatives are working for. Loan consolidation is extremely profitable for lenders, and it is often during exit counseling that students make their decisions regarding whether and with whom to consolidate their loans.

One tactic used by lenders to get access to students is co-branding. In this scheme, lenders pay universities for permission to use the schools' logos, colors, and so forth to market loans to students. In December 2007, Attorney General Andrew Cuomo announced a settlement with Student Financial Services, Inc., a loan-consolidation company based in Clearwater, Florida. The company had entered into agreements with colleges nationwide, fifty-seven of which were Division I schools. The list of schools involved with this one company is too long to be given here, but it included some very big names, such as Georgetown, Wake Forest, the University of Washington, Rutgers, Florida State, and many other well-known universities.[10]

Under these agreements, the universities were given kickbacks, a practice that was called revenue sharing. In return, the company gained the rights to use the schools' mascots, logos, colors, and team names to market their loans to students. Cuomo made clear his feelings about these arrangements. "When lenders use deceptive techniques to advertise their loans, they are playing a dangerous game with the student's future." He continued, "Student loan companies incorporate school insignia and colors into advertisements because they know students are more likely to trust a lender if its loan appears to be approved by their college. We cannot allow lenders to exploit this trust with deceptive, co-branded marketing. A student loan is a very serious financial commitment, and choosing the wrong loan can lead to devastating consequences."[11]

In the settlement that was reached, the company agreed to end all arrangements with the universities in question. In addition, the company agreed to adopt a code of conduct that effectively ended its ability to purchase rights to the schools' identifiers, such as their logos and insignias, in order to market loans to students. Further, the company may no longer give cash-based inducements or enter into agreements with sports marketing companies.

Professional Organizations

Another clear example of how the lines between lenders and universities are blurred is in the professional organizations that university financial aid administrators have formed. These organizations receive huge amounts of funding from student loan companies, and in many cases, staff members of lenders are appointed to leadership positions within the groups.

One illustration of this is the Rocky Mountain Association of Student Financial Aid Administrators. The purpose of this organization is ostensibly to serve the needs of students. In practice, this organization appears to be nothing more than a meeting ground for financial aid administrators and lenders. The sponsors of this organization are a veritable who's who of the student loan industry and include Sallie Mae, Nelnet, EdFund, and many others. Links on its Web site direct the viewer to lenders and guarantors, and of the fifty-six people listed in the group's leadership directory, ten work for student loan companies.

The National Association of Student Financial Aid Administrators (NASFAA) is, remarkably, far worse. It regularly holds high-priced events at exotic locations and solicits lenders heavily for its funding. For its 2008 conference in Orlando, NASFAA "gratefully acknowledges" no fewer than forty-one student lenders and guarantors. Further, it is a massive lobbying presence on Capitol Hill. Given NASFAA's nearly total financial dependence upon the lending industry, it is easy to understand why students' interests have been neglected in favor of lenders' interests. This bias is seen repeatedly in executive briefs issued by the organization, position papers issued by its members, and speeches given by its leadership. In particular, NASFAA leaders consistently call upon Congress to raise federal loan limits, and they lobby Congress to allow lenders to perform loan counseling for the students instead of having the colleges provide the information in an unbiased manner.[12]

Other Universities

While the total extent of the corruption of universities and university officials may never be known, there are already too many specific examples of corruption within higher education to enumerate in this book.

One interesting fact puts the breadth of this problem in some perspective. In June 2007 the Department of Education revealed that 1,412 colleges across the country had 80 percent or more of their students borrowing from one lender only. The list includes well-known universities such as Purdue, the University of Virginia, Seton Hall, and many others. Of these colleges, 531 were found to have 100 percent of their students' loans through a single lender.[13]

This prompted department officials to issue letters to 921 of the offending universities, giving them a friendly reminder that the schools had a responsibility to inform their students that they could choose any lender they wished; the letter also encouraged the schools to make sure that they were following federal rules and regulations.[14] The dollar value of the federally guaranteed loans at these 921 schools totaled $5.4 billion, representing hundreds of thousands of students.

The fact that so many institutions were funneling all, or nearly all, of their students toward a single lender is clear evidence that the students had, for all intents and purposes, no choice in their lenders. Further, the actions taken by the U.S. Department of Education are typical; in effect, they did as little as possible to actually fix the problem while at the same time seeming to make every attempt to fix it, thus preventing any public outcry that might jeopardize the system.

The fact that it took a state investigation, not a federal one, to expose these systemic defects is also telling. Certainly, were it not for the efforts of the New York State attorney general, these practices would be as prevalent as ever. Cuomo stated in an NPR interview that Congress should, at a minimum, revisit bankruptcy laws for student loans. For the sake of justice and decency, one hopes that some members of Congress will heed his advice.

CHAPTER SEVEN

The Grass Roots Awaken

Grassroots activities by student loan borrowers have begun to emerge since the amendments to the Higher Education Act in 1998. In the context of this book, *grassroots* refers to those organizations and collective activities executed by citizens affected by their student loans. These are not to be confused with initiatives created by existing professional advocacy organizations or with organizations that call themselves grassroots groups even though they have ties to and financial interests in the student loan industry. These are not true grassroots activities based on the original definition of the word, which has to do with organizations begun at a local level by the common people, not those developed by a major political force.

Initially, these activities were started by individual citizens who were desperate for relief. Over time, these individuals began to band together to share information and pursue joint research projects, and they finally coalesced into loose organizations that were formed for the purposes of exposing the problem to the public, gathering support, and, ultimately, compelling Congress to restore standard consumer protections to student loans.

Currently, the collective movement for student loan rights is at a very early stage of development, with fewer than five thousand citizens actively engaged. This is an incredibly small fraction of the ten to fifteen million citizens who are overwhelmed by student loan debt. Clearly, significant grassroots growth is required so that the people can convince Congress to address this issue meaningfully. This chapter describes the beginnings of these efforts and also charts a path for its success.

Weaknesses and Strengths

Grassroots activities to organize borrowers, expose the obvious problems, and ultimately redress the injustices associated with student loans would have been nearly impossible to undertake twenty years ago. There was no World Wide Web, and so it was far more difficult for borrowers to find one another and form effective groups. Even now, the barriers to inciting meaningful political action at the grassroots level are daunting. For one thing, facing large—and often insurmountable—student loan debt is a highly personal matter. Many debtors are too embarrassed or humiliated even to tell their immediate family members and close friends about their situation, let alone to join in a grassroots effort challenging the injustice of student lending laws.

A coordinator from New York, Heather Dunbar, put it this way: "People trapped under ridiculously large debt as a result of their student loans often have difficulties getting out of bed in the morning—convincing them to march in the streets and hold banners proclaiming their debt is about as easy as putting a cat in a bucket." The inherent reluctance of borrowers to take grassroots action because of their weakened financial position, aversion to risk, and shame is probably the most significant internal barrier to cohesive action.

From an organizational standpoint, the challenge of raising financial resources from the grassroots group members that are sufficient to compete with the lobbying interests on Capitol Hill is equally daunting. Given the financial predicament of those overwhelmed by student loan debt, this simply isn't going to happen, and other forces will have to be brought to bear on the problem.

Another internal difficulty: student loan borrowers are for the most part ordinary citizens trying to live normal lives. They are not inclined to pursue social justice and take on powers as great as the forces of the federal laws that have been erected to protect and sustain the federal student loan system. It is far easier for most to simply accept their fates as lifelong debtors and resign themselves to the wage garnishments, tax intercepts, and other collection activities that will inevitably ensue. One can see how easy it would be to consider all these challenges and then decide not to even attempt to organize a movement around the issue.

Perhaps the biggest external hurdle to achieving anything at the grassroots level is the long-standing national attitude toward college students in general. To many, the mere mention of the term *student* invokes a paternalistic response, and so any issue attached to it is disregarded. Moreover, an archetype exists in the nation's consciousness that connects student loan debt with irresponsibility. This is a result of well-publicized accounts of loan defaults in decades past in which students took out loans with no intention of ever paying them back and simply filed for bankruptcy after graduation. This perception was sufficiently strong that in the 1970s, Congress was convinced to remove bankruptcy protections from student loans. However, according to a March 2007 paper by John A. E. Pottow of the University of Michigan, this perception had a fatal flaw: "The fatal problem is that there are no empirical data to buttress the myth that students defraud creditors any more than other debtors."[1] In fact, it was shown that when student loans were dischargeable in bankruptcy, there was a less than 1 percent bankruptcy rate among student debtors.[2] Nevertheless, this misconception has been so often repeated that it is now indelibly etched in the public's mind.

Despite these various hurdles to organizing debtors, other factors explain the emergence of the student loan grassroots activities thus far. These will be critical to sustaining the continued growth and ultimate success of the efforts. People who analyze this debt system carefully will conclude that if there is to be any reasonable and equitable resolution to student loan debt, it will take a political solution, where the standard consumer protections that Congress removed from student loans are restored. Those without the financial means to pay the drastically higher amounts demanded of them have only one proactive option— namely, to stand up and speak out against their incomparable lack of consumer protections.

Student loan debtors are typically intelligent and educated individuals. Meaningful research, articulate communication, and insightful discussion with lawmakers, reporters, and the general public are required to effect change; this is another strength of the grassroots movement that can be brought to bear on the problem.

Also, with the maturing of communications technology, it has become far easier to seek out, find, and organize the people across the country who have been harmed by the student loan industry and who wish to band together for the purpose of effecting political change. The Internet is overwhelmed with advertisements promoted by student loan companies, and this deluge of marketing information makes it very difficult to find those engaged in the effort to fight for student loan justice; however, those individuals who are sufficiently dedicated and persistent will eventually find sites where like-minded individuals can congregate.

Finally, the problem of student debt is increasing, and at a rate proportional to the rise in the price of college tuition, which has been growing at double the rate of inflation for three decades. With the average undergraduate borrower leaving school with upward of twenty thousand dollars in student loan debt, and the average graduate borrower accruing forty-two thousand, inevitably there will be a tipping point beyond which the costs simply become too great to prevent broad public outcry. This fact alone virtually guarantees continued and increased grassroots activities for the foreseeable future.

StudentLoanJustice.org Is Created

It is in this environment that I founded StudentLoanJustice.org (SLJ) in March 2005. Initially, the organization was nothing more than a Web site that encouraged borrowers to tell their stories as accurately and honestly as possible. In the first month of operation, the site received five submissions from borrowers, and that was only after considerable effort was made to seek out these borrowers (who had posted on a legal resource Internet newsgroup) and convince them to tell their stories at SLJ.

Although initial submissions to the SLJ site were few, the span of the stories was intriguing, and it covered borrowers who had attended schools ranging from vocational institutions to Harvard. There was Rick, a laborer from California who'd decided to go back to school to learn automotive repair. The trade school he attended attempted to make him sign two separate promissory notes for what he was told would be one loan. Suspicious, Rick withdrew from classes and arranged for the cancellation of the loans. Five years later, owing to an IRS tax-refund offset, he realized that his loans had not been canceled and that the original fifteen-hundred-dollar note had grown to thirty-five hundred.

Then there was Petra, a Harvard graduate who left law school in 1986 with a little over forty thousand dollars in loans. After a prolonged period of unemployment and a denied forbearance, she reluctantly filed for bankruptcy. Her guarantor, the Illinois Student Assistance Commission, was paid 10 percent of the debt as a part of the bankruptcy settlement, and she was told that this was the end. Petra started over again, but the student loans were mysteriously revived. After the 1998 amendments to the Higher Education Act, student loan creditors began calling again and demanded payment in full for her loans, this time for the staggering amount of $152,000. Petra notes, "At the start of this story I mentioned that I am a single mother. Part of the reason for my divorce is this issue. My ex-husband couldn't handle the pressure and the threats of the lawsuit. He became enraged whenever I received a harassing phone call or notice letter demanding $152,000 in payment. It was too much for him to take."

By the summer of 2005, word had begun to spread about the Web site, and stories began to trickle in unsolicited. Again, the range of stories was compelling, but they all had in common an extraordinary increase in the amount being demanded from the loan holders as compared to the amount of the original loans. The site was also used as a platform to post research regarding lobbying activities, executive salary trends, and other information germane to the problem.

A significant number of submissions from citizens who had borrowed private student loans began to come in. These loans typically carried far higher interest rates than federally guaranteed loans, and bankruptcy protections had been removed (retroactively) from them as of October 17, 2005, as a part of the Bankruptcy Abuse Prevention and Consumer Protection Act of 2005.

The Importance of the Media

By the end of 2005, it had become apparent that the most effective way to make the public aware of the problem was through the media. Within weeks of the Web site's creation, the press had taken an interest in the stories on the site and in the research that was posted there. For example, Bethany McLean, a well-respected reporter for *Fortune* magazine, took a keen interest in the issue and was quick to see that the stock price of Sallie Mae had been exploding since 1998 and that the company did far better than others in the recession following the dot-com boom.

In December 2005, McLean published a five-page article on student loans that proved to be very important. In it, she described the massive profits being earned by lenders like Sallie Mae and covered a wide range of related topics, including the huge lobbying presence of Sallie Mae and the student loan industry on Capitol Hill and the rapid growth of private loans; she featured SLJ prominently in the piece. McLean and the staff at *Fortune* uncovered some astonishing information regarding these private loans; for example, they found a private student loan whose APR was an astonishing 28 percent.[3]

While the article met with intense and vehement criticism from Sallie Mae, the facts reported in the story were accurate. Shortly after this piece was published, SLJ membership grew by about three hundred members—still a tiny percentage of the number of borrowers caught in the student loan trap but nonetheless a significant step forward.

In March 2006, the *Baltimore Sun* agreed to publish a StudentLoanJustice.org op-ed that clearly described the lack of consumer protections for student loans and the human suffering that had resulted. While SLJ membership around that area increased only slightly following the piece, one submission from a man in Maryland describing the tragic circumstances surrounding his sister's self-inflicted death introduced a new reality to the fight.

When citizens are fleeing the country and committing suicide as a result of their student loan debt, all must agree that it is time to reconsider the whole notion of allowing our youth to assume more than token amounts of debt for their educations. To date, SLJ has received three stories of suicide from family members of student loan borrowers and hundreds of submissions from people who claim to be suicidal. We've also received dozens of submissions from people who have left the country, and hundreds from people who indicate that they are seriously considering it. Not because these people have committed crimes or because they are being persecuted for religious or other beliefs; it is solely because of the unendurable stress they are under as a result of their student loans.

In January 2006, Anya Kamenetz of the *Village Voice* published an important piece showing how Sallie Mae and the lending industry in general were making incredible profits from late fees charged to borrowers of both private and federally guaranteed student loans. The article also examined the obscenely large stock bonuses doled out to Sallie Mae executives, the potential for antitrust violations, and the huge amounts of money that Sallie Mae regularly poured into congressional coffers. SLJ members were interviewed and featured in the piece,[4] and membership increased a great deal as a result.

Then, in May 2006, a very significant story about Sallie Mae and the student loan industry ran on *60 Minutes.* It featured SLJ members, including Britt Napoli, the counselor in California who owed nearly triple what he had borrowed despite the fact that he had already repaid more than the amount of the original loan; Lynnae Brown, who was stuck repaying about a quarter of a million dollars on what began as a sixty-thousand-dollar loan; and Bill McLaughlin, a man whose CPA could not understand the astonishing amount that remained to be paid on his loans—Bill had originally borrowed thirty-eight thousand dollars and had repaid forty-eight thousand, yet he still owed about thirty-two thousand.

The *60 Minutes* segment aired as the top story on May 7, 2006, and shortly thereafter, StudentLoanJustice.org membership grew to well over a thousand members nationwide. The story sent ripples throughout academia and the student loan industry. While Sallie Mae issued a scathing criticism of the borrowers portrayed in the story and the quality of the reporting by CBS staff, the most significant fact of the matter is that Sallie Mae officers declined to be interviewed for the segment—stating that they didn't think they would get a fair shake.[5]

The *60 Minutes* piece gave the issue national prominence that proved hugely beneficial to the grassroots organizations. Within a week of the episode's airing, SLJ was contacted by both Ralph Nader and Michael Moore. Nader published a piece three days after the *60 Minutes* program aired in which he said that the corporate executives who had designed the student loan scheme should be given the top award for "shameless perversity." Moore asked to be connected with borrowers for potential inclusion in a documentary film, *Sicko,* which concentrated on the U.S. health-care system (ultimately the borrowers were not in the film). Although to date neither man has devoted significant resources to the student loan problem, it was encouraging to be contacted by citizens of the caliber of Nader and the audacity of Moore.

Other Media Coverage

The *Fortune* article proved that respected reporters were keenly interested in the issue, or at least that they became very interested when informed of the facts about student loans. SLJ decided that in order for this grassroots movement to succeed, the press would have to play a critical role. While SLJ continued to spend considerable effort researching the problem and attempting to convince Congress of the need to restore standard consumer protections to student loans, the organization spent an equal or perhaps greater amount of effort trying to interest regional and national publications and other media outlets in the issue.

In May 2006, Ken Moser, the president of the Adam Smith Society of California, published a scathing commentary on the lack of free-market forces in the student loan industry. The column specifically protested the fact that student loan borrowers are not allowed to refinance their debts after consolidation, regardless of whether there are lenders willing to accept less profit by charging the borrowers less to administer the loan. Given that the Adam Smith Society is one of the most conservative organizations in the world with regards to economics, this piece was highly noteworthy and significant.

The First Grassroots Legislative Achievement:
The Student Borrower Bill of Rights

A week after the *60 Minutes* piece, SLJ was asked to have a teleconference with Senator Clinton's education staff. During the conference, we discussed the appropriate elements of a Student Borrower Bill of Rights. The goals were to make sure that borrowers had crucial information before they took out their loans and to return standard consumer protections, including bankruptcy rights and refinancing rights, to the loans. Of the six suggestions SLJ made to the staff, three of them (bankruptcy rights, refinancing rights, and payment caps) made it into the text of the legislation.

The bill was introduced into the Senate on May 26, 2006 (S 511). While it didn't contain everything that SLJ members sought, it was certainly a step in the right direction and served as encouragement for the group. One of the Clinton staff members later sent an e-mail stating that it was the work of SLJ that had been the catalyst for the bill.[6] This was highly encouraging to the membership.

In March of 2006, Senator Dick Durbin contacted SLJ, and in June 2007 introduced S 1561, a bill to restore full bankruptcy protections for private student loans, loans that are not backed by the federal government and that often carry extraordinarily high interest rates.

Connie Martin, a constituent of Senator Durbin, was one of many SLJ members from Illinois. In 2002, at the age of twenty-five, Connie's son had decided to go to culinary school in Chicago; he borrowed about fifty-eight thousand dollars in private loans from Sallie Mae. The interest rate on his loans was 18 percent. His first payment was eleven hundred dollars a month—which was his entire monthly salary from the downtown eatery where he worked. His loan balance, including government-backed loans, stood at about a hundred thousand dollars, despite the thousands the family has already repaid.

In his speech on the Senate floor introducing the bill, Senator Durbin opened by describing the story of Connie Martin, an SLJ member since May 2006. He also had entered into the Senate record an important article published on the issue by the *Chicago Sun-Times*—an article that featured multiple SLJ members.[7] Again, this was a sterling example of how grassroots activities can contribute effectively to legislative change.

The Congressional Elections of 2006

Given that the ultimate goal of the grassroots effort for student loan justice is simply to convince Congress to restore standard consumer protections to student loans, the change in the majority control of both House and Senate in the fall of 2006 was of critical importance. The new majority held great promise for turning the legislation introduced by Clinton, Durbin, and others into a reality and for developing additional legislation to restore student loan protections.

In December 2006, the SLJ community decided to form a political action committee (PAC) as a counterbalance to the well-funded PACs controlled by the student loan industry; in January 2007, the PAC was established. SLJ accepted from the outset that the amount of money it raised would be a pittance compared to the millions of dollars spent every election cycle but that it was nevertheless an important and worthwhile step, if only for reasons of principle. As a companion grassroots act, SLJ members decided to travel the country on a bus tour, visiting as many members of the House and Senate Education committees as possible, both in their home districts and in Washington, D.C.

While some in the media questioned the move as a ridiculous effort by a "rabble rouser,"[8] others felt positively about the PAC and the bus tour. In fact, the *Boston Phoenix* did a feature story on the effort,[9] and more than five thousand dollars in donations was received before the trip began.

The trip covered forty-two states and more than twenty-three thousand miles. Of the seventy members of the Education committees, sixty were visited in their home districts. During the trip, the various scandals regarding the "unholy alliances" between the universities and student lenders broke in the mainstream media, and so SLJ members were featured in front-page stories in the *New York Times,* the *Washington Post,* and the *San Francisco Chronicle,* among many others newspapers. SLJ members gave talks at Cornell University, the University of North Carolina at Chapel Hill, and in many other locations, and the organization was invited to appear on local and national radio shows.

The bus tour cost about fifteen thousand dollars to execute (which is far less than the million dollars or more that Sallie Mae spends on their tour every year), but all the members felt that the money had been well spent. By the end of the 2007 tour, SLJ had established state coordinators for thirty-four states and was well on its way to having chapters in every state of the union.

Today there are SLJ chapters in every state, and they vary in size from a few dozen members to a few hundred. As time goes on and the problem worsens, the members of SLJ hope and expect that these volunteer chapters will serve as focal points for the continued growth and expansion of the organization.

Changing National Attitudes about Student Loans

It is significant that the national attitudes around student loan debt have changed recently. In years past, many citizens didn't give a second thought to the issue, likely as a result of long-standing paternalistic attitudes, lack of awareness of the problem, and the general reluctance of those affected to speak out. In recent years, however, owing to consistent and widespread media exposure, the problems with student loans have begun to seep into the public consciousness.

This shift in national awareness is difficult to quantify, but there are some indicators of change. Most notably, dozens of the nation's elite schools, including Princeton, Harvard, Amherst, Caltech, Davidson College, and the University of Pennsylvania, have committed to ending student loans either for all of their students or for those whose family incomes fall below certain thresholds.

Future Grassroots Development

The need for grassroots activities is only increasing. Recent U.S. Department of Education data indicates that defaults are far higher than the commonly advertised rates. Furthermore, contrary to what universities, lenders, guarantors, and even the Department of Education frequently claim, defaults may be increasing, not decreasing. A study tracking 1993 graduates found that for those borrowing more than fifteen thousand dollars, fully 20 percent had defaulted on their loans within ten years.[10] A more recent release from the Department of Education found that 10.6 percent of all borrowers leaving school in 2002 had defaulted within five years.[11] This damning default data certainly points toward a much larger and perhaps growing problem. Private loan borrowers are also defaulting at dramatically increasing rates. A number of student loan companies acknowledged that as a result of the credit crunch that began in 2007, there has been dramatically increased default rates for their private loans. While the hard numbers are difficult, if not impossible, to determine, Sallie Mae's top brass stated in a conference call with investors that the company was setting aside nearly $600 million for bad loans in the private market and that they would be more selective in the future when making private loans.[12]

Clearly, the groundwork has been laid for a significant surge in activism around this issue. In addition to the Student-LoanJustice.org organization, several other activist groups have formed, and their numbers are growing. They include StudentLoanSlave.com, SallieMaeBeef.com, JoesDebt.com, and a host of Internet newsgroups. There are also dozens of similarly focused blogs started by individual citizens. While this is encouraging from a grassroots perspective, much work needs to be done. There are at least ten million citizens overwhelmed by student loan debt, and yet there are currently fewer than five thousand people who are actively engaged in bringing about a solution.

One critically important but currently absent sector of grassroots activity is at the university level. Unless a military draft is instituted, the most compelling issue for students has to be the overwhelming cost of college and the predatory lending environment that supports it. Students need to realize how severely they are being exploited, and then they need to speak out against it loudly and forcefully. Over the last four decades, colleges and universities have been sitting in the catbird seat, raising their tuition, fees, and other costs almost at will, knowing that students gladly sign up for increased loans to subsidize their education. Until they hear from the students—strongly, loudly, and consistently—the colleges will likely continue to operate as they have for years now, taking advantage of the very population they profess to support.

CHAPTER EIGHT

Solutions

Citizens, student advocacy groups, and states' attorneys general have begun to make it clear that monumental changes are critically needed for student loans, and Congress is beginning to respond. Widespread publicity showing how standard consumer protections were removed from student loans, how banks and universities actively engaged in improper and exploitive relationships with lenders and students for the sake of monetary gain, and how student loan debt has affected the U.S. population has changed the national discourse on the subject. The rhetoric on Capitol Hill has finally turned to favor the consumers, not the banks, and the average citizen is now aware that this type of debt has serious, grave implications.

Since 2006, significant student loan legislation has been introduced, and some notable improvements have even been signed into law by President Bush. This is an encouraging first step. Make no mistake, however: thus far, legislation proposed for the reinstatement of standard consumer protections for student loans has not progressed anywhere close to the point of being signed into law, and indeed much of it has stalled or been abandoned. Student loans still remain absent of standard consumer protections, but at least the groundwork has been laid for the future. Even Sallie Mae representatives have stated publicly, in a congressional hearing, that it may be time to reexamine bankruptcy laws for student loans.

This chapter discusses recent legislation, proposes additional legislation that should be considered, and briefly touches on potential solutions for what is truly the overwhelming problem of higher education: the astonishing rise in price.

The College Cost Reduction Act of 2007

On September 27, 2007, President Bush signed into law the College Cost Reduction and Access Act (PL 110–84). Touted as the most significant higher education legislation since the GI Bill, this law mandates significant improvements for students. The new law provides for a halving of interest rates for future undergraduate students on the subsidized portion of their federally guaranteed loans, increases the maximum Pell grant amount slightly, and cuts lender subsidies significantly and guarantor collection fees slightly.

While this legislation provides tangible benefits for current and future students, it does very little for those who are already buried under unmanageable student loan debt, especially those defaulted borrowers whose loan balances have doubled, tripled, or even grown by an entire order of magnitude as a result of unreasonable collection charges and other fees. In fact, it could be argued that while the cuts in lender subsidies will certainly benefit the federal government, they will actually have an adverse effect on people who have already seen their loan balances escalate: the lenders will work more aggressively to make profits in other areas in order to compensate for the shortfall caused by the subsidy cuts.

From the perspective of defaulted borrowers, the bill's most important aspect was a provision for loan forgiveness after ten years of public service. This was touted by some public policy advocates as a potential solution for defaulted borrowers whose loan balances have spiraled out of control due to penalties and fees. However, for a number of reasons, the public service plan is largely unacceptable for the purpose of clearing defaulted student loan debt.

First, assuming the borrower successfully finds and maintains public service employment for ten years, under current law, the amount forgiven would be treated as taxable income. Given that most defaulted borrowers have loan balances that far exceed the amount they originally borrowed and that their loan balances are likely to increase significantly during the remaining term of the loans, the amount of taxes they would have to pay immediately after the end of the term would likely be astronomical, often more than the original loan balance.

Second, the borrowers would be forced to rehabilitate their loans in order to qualify for the program. This entails signing a new promissory note, thus legitimizing all the penalties and fees that caused their loan balances to increase dramatically. Moreover, throughout the term of the repayment, the loan balance will likely increase; if the borrower should happen to experience a financial windfall, it would probably be consumed by this onerous debt.

There is a larger issue to consider here: this program smacks of indentured servitude. Being relegated to working in a specific field for the sole purpose of retiring one's unreasonably large student loan debt is a severe restriction on a citizen's freedom. This sentiment is felt most strongly by those borrowers in their forties, fifties, and beyond who have no wish to quit their current jobs and find new ones in the public sector for the sole purpose of retiring their exploded student loan debt.

David Aigaki, the chiropractor in Texas who has been relegated to driving trucks because the state had revoked his license to practice medicine due to his defaulted loans, raises some critical questions regarding the new legislation.

I originally borrowed $75,000. They are now demanding about $400,000 in payment. I suppose that I could quit my job, take a cut in pay, learn a new field, and take a job at a nonprofit somewhere for ten years, and give up 15 percent of my income along the way, but at the end of the day, I'll probably owe half a million. What is the tax on that? I'm fifty years old now; where am I going to find a hundred-plus thousand dollars—on top of what I will have already paid—to pay these people off after all is said and done? I don't want to die in debt, but at this point, it's looking like either that, or the tax hit at the end will put me into an early grave anyway, so I can't win—the U.S. government has seen to that.

There is another issue for borrowers who have seen their loan balances explode, and it is one of trust. Many borrowers who were defaulted on their loans feel they were defaulted improperly in the first place. Others accept responsibility for the default, but they see clearly that the system as designed is heavily tilted in favor of the lenders, and they feel abused by years of ruthless collection tactics and their lack of recourse under the law, so they no longer have any faith in government on this issue. These borrowers have been bullied for so many years by the system, they have no desire to enter into long-term contracts on the debts with a party they do not trust. After all, Congress retroactively removed bankruptcy protections from student loan debt, so what assurances do borrowers have that the rules will not change yet again in the middle of the game, depending on the whims of Congress?

To be sure, this program may be attractive for recent graduates whose loans have not ballooned due to default. However, in the view of nearly all defaulted borrowers who have studied this program, the plan is completely unacceptable, and they see it as a cheap attempt by Congress to forgo the reinstatement of the standard consumer protections that have been taken away from student loans.

The Student Loan Sunshine Act of 2007

In May 2007, the House of Representatives voted overwhelmingly (414–3) to approve the Student Loan Sunshine Act. This act was in response to the attorney general's investigation that revealed widespread corruption within the industry, and it called for sweeping reforms of the relationships between the lenders and the universities. Under this act, colleges were required to make full disclosure of any special arrangements between lenders and institutions of higher education. The legislation also banned lenders from offering gifts worth more than ten dollars to college employees, including travel, lodging, and entertainment, and banned lenders from providing in-kind services to college financial aid offices. The legislation further required full disclosure of the reasons why an institution of higher education selected a lender for its preferred-lender list, including any special arrangements the lender had with the school.

Again, this was welcome legislation, and it will certainly provide for more education for the borrowers prior to their taking out student loans. It does not, however, offer any benefit for those citizens who have already taken out loans.

Bankruptcy Protections

While no one ever wants to file for bankruptcy, the reasons for bankruptcy protections are well founded. Bankruptcy protection affords citizens with insurmountable debts a legal mechanism for resolving their debts and then continuing on to be productive citizens. Most consumers who file for bankruptcy do so for reasons beyond their control. This is seen by most as a critically important freedom to have, and it serves as a protection against the human rights abuses that frequently occurred for debtors in centuries past, including slavery, indentured servitude, and debtors' prison. It is critical that a nation provide its citizens with bankruptcy protections in order to encourage and foster entrepreneurship, risk-taking, and creativity. Notable Americans such as Thomas Jefferson and Henry Ford went bankrupt multiple times during their lives, yet they contributed greatly to society through their creative and social endeavors.

The rationale for the removal of bankruptcy protections for federally guaranteed student loans was largely predicated on undocumented anecdotal examples of students who filed for bankruptcy immediately upon graduation. In fact, most of the anecdotal incidents involved credit-card debt, not student loan debt. Instances of this type of activity were widely reported in the media, and so, in 1978, Congress added a seven-year repayment requisite before student loans could be discharged in bankruptcy. The amendments to the Higher Education Act in 1998 went much further and removed bankruptcy protections completely for the majority of borrowers.

Interestingly, the language that exempted student loans from bankruptcy discharge in the 1978 overhaul of bankruptcy laws, an addition that reportedly came up "at the last minute,"[1] was opposed by both the primary cosponsor of the bill, Rep. Don Edwards, and the chairman of the House Subcommittee on Postsecondary Education, Rep. James O'Hara. Edwards's opposition was strong. He said that Congress was "fighting a 'scandal' which exists primarily in the imagination."[2]

Moreover, the statistics on bankruptcy filings painted a far different picture than the one used as a premise for removing bankruptcy protections from student loans. Examples of people graduating from college and then promptly filing for bankruptcy protections for the sole purpose of erasing student loan debt simply did not occur in numbers large enough to warrant such draconian legislation. In fact, it was shown by the Government

Accountability Office that prior to the 1978 legislation, less than 1 percent of federally guaranteed student loans were discharged in bankruptcy proceedings.[3] Thus, the initial basis for the removal of bankruptcy protections is highly suspect and evidently without firm grounding in fact.

Another rationale given for the removal of bankruptcy protections from student loans is that the federal government guarantees these loans. However, there is no precedent for this; there are no other federal loan guarantees in existence in the United States—secured or unsecured—that are subject to bankruptcy exemptions. From Farm Loans to FEMA loans to SBA loans to all government loans and government loan guarantees, not a single one other than the student loan is exempt from bankruptcy discharge.

In general, higher education provides the nation with a public benefit, and so student loans, at least in theory, should be more beneficial to the borrower in terms of consumer protections than loans that cover items that do not contribute to the public good, such as credit cards and gambling. Yet we find that exactly the opposite is true. For the purposes of bankruptcy, student loans are in a class with criminal debt, unpaid child support, and delinquent taxes. It should be obvious to any logical thinker that this is wrong.

For private student loans, the lending industry argued that removal of bankruptcy protections would allow individuals with lower credit scores to have more access to funds because they, the lenders, would relax the underwriting criteria. However, two years after Congress removed bankruptcy protections for private loans, no evidence could be found to show that the lenders followed through with their promise (this information is based on disclosures by the largest private lenders in their prospectuses for private student loan securitizations). A study conducted by Mark Kantrowitz, publisher of www.FinAid.org, found that since the removal of bankruptcy protections for private loans, in 2005, the percentage of borrowers with low credit scores receiving private loans from, for instance, Sallie Mae increased by a mere 0.2 percent.[4]

Sallie Mae Acknowledges Need for Bankruptcy Protections

In 2007 there was a public and congressional outcry over the removal of bankruptcy protections for private loans, and even Sallie Mae executives conceded that perhaps bankruptcy protections needed to be revisited. In June of that year, Sallie Mae spokesperson Martha Holler told Paul Basken of the *Chronicle of Higher Education,* "We agree that it may be appropriate to revisit how to handle private student loans in bankruptcy."[5] Similarly, Conway Casillas, Sallie Mae's public affairs director, told *Time* magazine in September 2007 that it might be appropriate to revert to the previous laws regarding bankruptcy of student loans, where discharge was possible after a seven-year repayment history by the borrower.[6]

These acknowledgments from Sallie Mae are hugely important. After all, the Sallie Mae lobbying machine went to great lengths to support legislation that took these rights away in the first place. Indeed, a December 2006 internal strategy memo regarding federal government relations from Sallie Mae made that was public in 2007 showed that of the seven objectives for the company on this front, the second was to "protect private credit economics (including bankruptcy)."[7]

Canada Relaxes Bankruptcy Restrictions

The Canadian government changed bankruptcy protections for student loans at approximately the same time as the U.S. Congress. In 1997 a two-year window was placed on the debt after the student graduated, during which time the loans were not dischargeable. In 1998 this window was extended to ten years. In 2007, however, legislation was approved and is currently pending passage that would reduce the ten-year window to seven years for all borrowers and to five years for those facing hardships.[8]

Bankruptcy Legislation for Federally Guaranteed Student Loans

In May 2006, Senator Hillary Clinton (D-NY) introduced the Student Borrower Bill of Rights Act of 2007 (S 511). This legislation had a plethora of important modifications to the Higher Education Act, not least of which was the reinstatement of bankruptcy protections for student loans. The act provided for the return of bankruptcy protections for federally guaranteed loans, with the restriction that borrowers be in repayment status for seven years, effectively rolling back the law to pre-1998 conditions. The legislation was reintroduced in March 2007.

The Student Borrower Bill of Rights prefaced its language regarding bankruptcy by stating that the Bankruptcy Abuse Prevention and Consumer Protection Act of 2005 (BAPCPA) affords sufficient protections to prevent fraud and abuse in the carefully regulated discharge of student loans in bankruptcy.

There are two problems with this legislation. First, it applies only to loans made on or after the enactment of the legislation. Second, if a borrower is in such desperate financial condition that a bankruptcy filing is warranted, having to wait as long as seven years to file does nothing for the immediate financial distress. In other words, this legislation provides no relief for borrowers who have already seen their student loan debt explode. Congress needs to enact legislation that restores full bankruptcy protections for all student loans and all borrowers, regardless of when the loans were made, and puts the loans on an equal basis with all other types of consumer credit. It is hoped that there will be significant attention paid to arguments made by such experts as Elizabeth Warren, John Pottow, Deanne Loonin, and others on this issue.

Bankruptcy Legislation for Private Student Loans

Senator Dick Durbin (D-IL) introduced legislation in June 2007 that would restore bankruptcy protections for private student loans. Senator Chris Dodd announced a plan in November 2007 that would similarly reinstate bankruptcy protections for private loans.

The fact that these loans were exempted from bankruptcy discharge in the first place was a testament to the lobbying prowess of the student loan industry with the Congress of 2005, and it had little rational basis except for what turned out to be the false promise by the lending industry that the bankruptcy exemption would allow greater access to higher education for individuals with low or no credit scores. Moreover, given that lenders are adopting more stringent credit underwriting criteria in response to the sub-prime mortgage credit crisis, there is no longer any need for a bankruptcy exception. Unfortunately, the Durbin legislation has not progressed far, and there are indications that the bill may be quietly abandoned.[9] Senator Dodd ended his presidential campaign in January 2008. It is not known if his plan will move forward in light of his withdrawal.

In February 2008, Rep. Danny Davis (D-IL) introduced an amendment to the Higher Education Act Reauthorization to restore limited bankruptcy protections for private student loans. This amendment, like the Durbin legislation, was seen by student advocates as a long-overdue correction to language that the 2005 Republican Congress had slipped into the bankruptcy bill that made private student loans (loans not guaranteed by the federal government) nondischargeable in bankruptcy.

The amendment apparently passed by a voice vote, but Buck

McKeon (R-CA) called for a recorded vote, and there was a delay. During this time, the banks and their lobbying machines went to work. By the time the votes were cast, the amendment no longer had the necessary support, and it failed.

It turned out that many Blue Dog Democrats had voted against the amendment after they were heavily lobbied by the Consumer Bankers Association and other student loan interests on the Hill. Fully twenty-nine of the thirty-seven Blue Dog members voted to kill this amendment, which were easily enough voters to make the difference between the initiative's being a success or a failure.[10]

Refinancing Rights

It is a basic free-market principle that if there is a lender who is willing to charge lower interest or otherwise give a better deal to a borrower, that borrower should be able to refinance the debt with the new lender. According to federal law, however, a student who has consolidated his or her federally guaranteed loans can never leave that lender for a more competitive bank. This captivity is a major source of distress for borrowers, many of whom were locked into extremely high interest rates with inferior customer service. For a brief period, there was a convoluted mechanism available through which a borrower could transfer his loans into the Direct Loan Program and then back out and go to a private lender under more favorable terms, and millions of borrowers took advantage of this procedure while they could. However, in 2006, after intense lobbying by Sallie Mae and other companies, Congress closed this loophole. Tom Joyce, a Sallie Mae spokesman, commented that this anti-competitive move would make smaller lenders think twice about getting into the student loan business.

Senator Clinton's Student Borrower Bill of Rights also called for the right of students to refinance (or reconsolidate) their federally guaranteed student loans. Surprisingly, no Republican members of Congress have stepped forward to call for similar refinancing rights. This lack of commitment to free-market enterprise among some members of Congress may suggest a conflict of interest for those whose campaign coffers are filled by individuals who would not benefit from such a free market.

Future Legislation

The current legislative efforts regarding student loans are significant, but there are still key areas for improvement. First, a borrower's ability to practice in his or her chosen field should not be encumbered by student loan debt. Currently, many states regularly suspend professional licenses as a result of defaulted student loan debt, which only serves to compound the financial difficulties being faced by the borrowers and does nothing to benefit the public. How does Congress expect a doctor to repay medical school debt if he is unable to practice medicine, or a lawyer to pay back law school loans if she is unable to practice law? Suspending their licenses is counterproductive. Legislation should be introduced that does away with this practice entirely.

George, a registered nurse in Texas, can't understand the current law. He wants to repay a fair amount for his defaulted loans, but his nursing license was suspended, and so his hands are effectively tied. "This is completely upside down: They demand that we pay an outrageous amount on these loans, and then they turn around and force us to work at McDonald's to do it. It seems like some kind of trick to keep us paying their penalties and fees for the rest of our lives. There has to be a fair way to do this, but this isn't it. I've never been so hamstrung by my own government, who I served faithfully during years of military service."

Legislation that prevents lenders from "double tapping" defaulted borrowers needs to be introduced. Double tapping occurs when the original lender owns the collection company that is used to collect the increased amount of the defaulted loans, which are now under contract either with the state guarantor or the federal government. In effect, this gives the lending company a perverse incentive to default the borrower; the lender gets paid nearly the full balance of the defaulted loan but also stands to make significant extra income from the collection of the defaulted loan, the amount of which has escalated dramatically due to penalties and fees. If the lender was unable to collect the loan when it held title to that loan, how does the guarantor agency expect the lender to be able to collect the loan on the agency's behalf? This provides the lender with a clear conflict of interest and encourages them to fall short in their initial collection efforts. Congress should pass legislation that bans guarantor agencies from retaining lenders (and their subsidiaries) to collect on loans to which those lenders previously held title.

Further, it is abhorrent that many of our elderly and disabled citizens have their Social Security and disability income garnished by the federal government. Marilynn Piszczek, of Riverside, California, attended the International Flight Academy in Ontario, California, in the 1980s. At the time, she believed that the loan documents she was signing were for grants. She was shocked when she began receiving notices of default; to make matters worse, she had been terminated from her job due to a lung condition.

Marilynn is now sixty-six years old and derives the majority of her income from Social Security. According to Marilynn, "Since the Social Security cost-of-living increase, the student loan people have taken more of my monthly check and I am still stuck for all of my rent or trying to figure out where it is to come from. I cannot walk anymore and cannot get in and out of my house that way and cannot get a ramp built for my power chair—and they are taking a bigger lump of my monthly income and do not try to answer any questions from me or anyone else. Sometimes I hope that maybe one day they or someone in their family will get this treatment and then they won't get out of it either."

Repayment Limits for Federally Guaranteed Student Loans

While restoring bankruptcy protections, statutes of limitations, refinancing rights, and other standard consumer protections to student loans is of critical importance, it is also highly desirable that Congress implement upper limits for repayment of federally guaranteed loans, regardless of the past repayment history of the borrower. The astonishing level of debt increase that typically befalls student borrowers with no recourse can be crippling for citizens for whom bankruptcy is not an option due to personal considerations. There needs to be an upper limit on how much these people should be forced to pay on their loans, particularly if they faced default or egregious fees and penalties during repayment.

In other words, regardless of what happens during repayment of a loan, the borrower should never be forced to pay more than a certain amount over a certain time period. This type of repayment cap would go a long way to ensure that citizens who are not in a position to file for bankruptcy have at least some protection from exploitation by the industry. Again, Senator Clinton's Student Borrower Bill of Rights addresses this issue and calls upon the Senate to study what reasonable repayment caps might look like over ten- and twenty-five-year periods.

Interest rate caps for private student loans would also be very useful. Given the usurious interest rates that are currently being charged for private student loans, approaching 30 percent in some cases, one would hope that federal regulations could be established to prevent usury by setting maximum interest rates.

Reducing the Price of College

Although the critical and immediate need is to restore standard consumer protections and curb collection powers for student loans, an underlying problem has not been addressed: the costs and, ultimately, the price that colleges demand of students, whether in the form of loans or in direct payments by the students and their families. As a society, we should reconsider our decision to place so much of the financial burden of higher education on our citizens in the first place. The current higher education funding framework has proven to be obscenely inflationary by its very nature, and it is fed largely by the naïveté, vulnerability, and optimism of the nation's students. As a result, we must now brace ourselves for the impact this will inevitably have on the well-being of these citizens and their families for years to come.

Dr. Larry Leslie, who was a Penn State professor in the 1970s, noticed this disturbing trend and wrote about it at the time.[11] Today, even in hindsight, Dr. Leslie is certain that his concern was well founded. Now at the University of Georgia, he comments, "My current views regarding college costs center around the failure of state governments to adequately fund their colleges and universities and the federal government's policy of promoting student aid at the expense of institutional aid. It is these factors, in my view, that largely have moved us in the direction of higher tuitions and related costs. The discussion of the past two decades or so regarding grants v. loans would largely be moot if governments had continued to fund institutions."

He continues, "The arguments for the high tuition–high aid policy that has guided higher education funding over the past thirty-plus years was doomed from the beginning, as it turned the support of higher education into a means-test-based policy that has greatly damaged the support of the middle class, who now pay their high taxes, then must turn around and pay high costs for their children."

It is time to seriously consider a return to the days of low-tuition, government-funded colleges and universities. This would obviously make higher education much more accessible to the general public and would also obviate the need for the overwhelming, complex, and expensive layers of bureaucracy that accompany the entire student aid system.

Of course, the taxpayer should not have to pay for the excesses that have crept into our nation's higher education institutions. However, one does not have to look far within today's schools to see areas where most institutions of higher learning could cut costs significantly. Fancy gyms, student unions, expensive nonacademic programs, administrative salaries, exorbitant salaries and bonuses for athletic coaches, and other capital projects that go well beyond the classic paradigm of teaching and learning are obvious areas.

It is beyond the scope of this book to delve more deeply into the proposition of returning to institutional aid over student aid, but it is hoped that this recommendation is given serious consideration by the public stakeholders in our higher education system going forward.

Reducing Degree Requirements

One interesting idea that has been proposed to lower the cost of college is the concept of reducing course requirements for degrees, and thereby reducing the cost of those degrees. Notably, Mayor Richard Daley of Chicago suggested in September 2007 that universities should consider cutting course loads in half. He commented, "They should cut half the courses. It would cut the cost down tremendously. What are the basic courses that you need in college? Cut some of the unnecessary courses out." This would reduce administrative overhead and let students graduate sooner.[12]

Indeed, it is taking longer for students to graduate. In 2003, the Education Trust found that only 37 percent of undergraduate students completed their degrees within four years.[13] While cutting course loads by half is an extreme measure that would likely shortchange students' educations, the sentiment could be worth further discussion, particularly in today's ultra-high-cost environment.

It took more than a decade for Congress to take away the standard consumer protections that we take for granted with every other type of loan. One can't expect them to be returned overnight. However, the work has been done to ready the nation for significant change, and legislators can no longer overlook the astonishing rise in price of a college education, and they cannot ignore the real human suffering that is taking place as a result. One can only hope that Congress and the executive branch will act quickly, both to improve the system in the future and to address the more immediate problems that the student loan system has already caused.

CHAPTER NINE

Practical Advice for Borrowers

There is a compelling need to return standard consumer protections to student loans. There is also a critical need to reduce the out-of-pocket cost of a college education. These are large issues that are in the nation's best interest to address, and it is hoped that this book will help stimulate changes.

Student borrowers and their families need to educate themselves about their options and take an active role as consumers throughout the entire financial aid process. It is only by doing the necessary research beforehand that the chance of encountering problems can be minimized. Simply trusting the university financial aid offices and lenders is not enough. From career colleges to Ivy League universities, many institutions of higher learning tend to serve their own interests first rather than the best interests of the students.

This chapter provides some practical advice. This guidance comes from research on the subject and interviews with experts in the field, and it also relates some hard lessons learned from borrowers who have gone through the default process and had some success.

Before Choosing a University

The best advice for incoming and prospective students is obvious: Don't borrow. This advice is easy to give but much harder to follow, especially since nearly 70 percent of college students leave school with student loans. However, it is worthwhile to keep this as a goal, even if it cannot be completely met. Students should exhaust all non-loan financial aid opportunities to the greatest extent possible. Actively pursue scholarships, work-study, grants, and other forms of aid that do not require repayment.

When considering which college to attend, the student should consider the school's cost as a primary factor. Students should apply to multiple universities and carefully weigh the financial implications of each. In many, if not most, instances, a student should not be overly impressed by a university's claim to be the best in a given field of study. Students should look at the schools' graduation rates, average length of attendance (for example, does the average student graduate in four years, five years, or even six years?), default rates for graduates, and any other longitudinal data obtainable. Schools often have much of this information available upon request.

Mark Kantrowitz, publisher of the FinAid Web site, recommends that in addition to the usual assortment of colleges, students should apply to financial aid safety schools. A financial aid safety school is a college that a student can both get in to and pay for, even if that student received no financial aid. He also recommends borrowing a total amount that is no more than your expected starting salary. "If you find yourself borrowing too much, consider switching to a less expensive college."

In general, be very, very wary of new schools that have no track record and any for-profit schools, particularly those that advertise on television. Not all for-profit colleges are bad, but prospective students need to investigate them carefully. Culinary schools, photography schools, chiropractic colleges, cosmetology schools, truck-driving schools, flight schools, and other specialized institutes have notoriously bad track records in the StudentLoanJustice.org community, and these schools can cost tens of thousands of dollars, even more in some instances. Often, these schools are nonaccredited, and so students applying for loans to go there have no choice but to take out high-interest, private loans. These schools have an alarming tendency to close and leave students with the bills but no degrees or valuable education. One can often find a less expensive and better education at a public college.

A good example of this is the case of Silver State Helicopters. This flight school, with thirty-three campuses nationwide, closed its doors and filed for bankruptcy in February 2008.[1] Many of its 2,700 students, who had paid in advance through private loans, were left with no education and no degrees. Private student loans do not have a closed school discharge like federal student loans. The company listed its assets at fifty thousand dollars at the time of filing, and they had more than ten million dollars in debt. The students will likely see nothing for all of their efforts to get an education with Silver State.

Christopher Heatly is one such victim of Silver State. He took out sixty thousand dollars in loans from a private lender but received only limited instruction and no certificate prior to the school's closing. He cannot file for bankruptcy on the debt, since private student loans are not dischargeable. Chris says he was impressed with the company's ranking in *Inc.* magazine as one of the country's five hundred fastest-growing companies, and he had faith that they were solvent. He does not know what he will do.

In general, students and their families need to be very wary, cautious, and mindful of the pitfalls of higher education, and base their actions on as much knowledge as possible. Often, the worst mistakes are made before stepping foot on campus, and these decisions can have serious and long-term consequences.

After Acceptance to College

After students receive their financial aid offer letters, very few try to negotiate with their schools to minimize the amount of loans they will need to take out. However, this can be worth the effort. The prestige of the institutions tends to make students think that they need the schools much more than the school needs them, but this is not the case. Prospective and current students should take every opportunity to negotiate more favorable financial aid packages with their schools' financial aid offices.

The trick to a successful negotiation is knowing how to do it. Mr. Kantrowitz says that schools are not like car dealerships, where "bluff and bluster" can get you a better deal. Rather, you should provide the college with complete information about any unusual financial situations, such as anything that differentiates your family from the typical family and any change in financial circumstances that have occurred since the previous year. Examples of unusual circumstances include unreimbursed medical and dental expenses, casualty losses, job loss, death of a wage earner, volatile annual income, and one-time events that are not reflective of ability to pay during the award year. If one of your other colleges provided a better financial aid offer, it's often a sign that you provided key information to that college and not to the others. Ask the college for a professional-judgment review, sometimes called a special-circumstances review, and provide them with documentation of any unusual circumstances. Also, if you are bringing in a lot of outside scholarships (which triggers an overaward), you can sometimes ask the college to reduce your loans before touching the grants.

Mr. Kantrowitz also recommends comparing colleges based on out-of-pocket cost. "To calculate the out-of-pocket cost, omit the loans from the financial aid package and subtract what's left from the cost of attendance. Out-of-pocket cost reflects the amount you will need to pay from savings and current income, and future income in the form of loans. Out-of-pocket cost tends to correlate well with cumulative debt at graduation," he said.

Once the student has made the decision to attend one university or another and is satisfied that every attempt has been made to minimize the amount of loans required, the next step is choosing a lender. While the university will probably have a list of preferred lenders to choose from, students should be wary of these lists. As detailed in previous chapters, the reasons for these lenders being on these lists are not always related to the value of the loans for the students. Rather, lenders often have preexisting arrangements with the universities that are beneficial to the universities but not necessarily to the students. Preferred-lender lists may be good starting points, but the student needs to do research rather than just pick the first name he sees, which is all too often the case.

Students should contact as many lenders as is feasible to determine which lender offers the best terms on the loans. While federally guaranteed loans have maximum interest rates that lenders can charge to students, there can be other terms that are more beneficial for the students, such as interest rate reductions for on-time payments and reductions for automatic payments. Students should assess all of these benefits. The *Greentree Gazette* is a student loan trade magazine that publishes a comprehensive survey of these benefits and serves as one guide students may wish to use. FinAid.org also does a comprehensive evaluation that is worthwhile.

The Dangers of Private Loans

Private student loans have exploded to rival federally guaranteed loans in the industry. In a few short years, they have grown to encompass nearly a quarter of the entire industry, and the airwaves are saturated with ads for these dangerous debt instruments. Many students make the mistake of applying for private loans instead of federal loans because they are attracted to the ease and quickness of the application process. However, the ease of applying can come at a great, often ruinous cost. Interest rates can be astronomical, and, like federal loans, the bankruptcy protections for private loans are extremely limited. This makes the lenders far less willing to negotiate with students facing financial difficulty.

Students often fall into the trap of these private loans and are led to believe that they are standard loans. Many do not understand the terms of the loans when they sign, and they find out only after it is too late that they agreed to interest rates of 18 percent, 20 percent, or more. The interest on these loans alone is sometimes more than half a student's income after graduation. Moreover, parents often cosign these loans, and this puts their assets and credit scores at great risk.

The stories that have been received at the StudentLoanJus tice.org Web site from private loan holders are increasing dramatically, and the situations are truly heartbreaking at times. Given that private loans account for more than 25 percent of the entire student loan market, it should come as absolutely no surprise that in 2007 borrowers began defaulting on these loans in record numbers.

Jason Clark originally borrowed about thirty thousand dollars to attend the Pennsylvania Culinary Institute. His lender, Sallie Mae, was recommended by the school. He says he never saw a promissory note after filling out the application, and he definitely never agreed to the interest rate or to any variable interest rate. Six months after graduation, Jason was alarmed to see that his interest rate was at 13 percent. He says he was told by the financial aid staff at the school that interest rates would be "reasonable," which he assumed meant that the interest would be below 10 percent, perhaps well below. He was wrong. His monthly payments, $635 per month, were unaffordable, and Jason paid to use a six-month deferment. When his deferment ended, he was astounded to find that his interest rate had increased to 18 percent, and his monthly payments were now $739 per month.

Jason has two jobs, lives with his parents, and still can only barely afford the monthly payments on his loans. He estimates that over the next fifteen years, assuming that he somehow manages to maintain his payment schedule, he will pay about a hundred and fifteen thousand dollars for his original thirty-thousand-dollar loan.

Use Federal Loans First

Federal loans are always, without question, the more beneficial types of loan. While private lenders advertise heavily on campus, on the radio, and on television, private loans are never better than federal loans. Federal loans always have lower interest rates (set by Congress). Many are subsidized, so that the interest is paid while the student is in school. Federally guaranteed loans also have more flexible repayment options and federally mandated deferment and forbearance programs, which private loans do not offer.[2] Also, for federal loans, there are at least some circumstances in which loans can be forgiven, including the death of the student, total and permanent disability of the student borrower, school closure, and others. Currently, federal annual loan limits are as follows: $3,500 for freshmen; $4,500 for sophomores; $5,500 each for juniors and seniors; and $8,500 per year for graduate students.[3]

If a student's financial aid package falls short of covering costs by using just federal loans, then that student should give serious consideration to attending a less expensive college. The credit crunch of 2007–2008 caused a significant tightening of underwriting standards for private loans, and so it is by no means certain that a private loan application will be approved (incidentally, this is despite the rhetoric of the lending industry prior to the 2005 bankruptcy bill that exempted private educational loans from bankruptcy discharge). A student faced with the choice of either taking out private loans (often with his or her parents as cosigners) or attending a different school should give very serious consideration to the latter choice.

More broadly, the student should consider whether taking out any educational loans, private or federal, is worth it. The astonishing lack of consumer protections associated with each type of debt should be considered carefully against the range of possible financial outcomes for the student as a result of pursuing the degree of his or her choice. There are a number of reputable resources online for financial planning for college. While most if not all of these have financial arrangements with lending companies, students may benefit from examining these sites. FinAid.org is one such site, and it offers a range of financial planning tools that can help a student plan for college.

Learn about the Impact of Defaulting on Loans Prior to Obtaining Them

Most defaulted borrowers had no idea that student loans could not be refinanced after consolidation, were largely exempt from bankruptcy discharge, and had no statutes of limitations for their collections. The vast majority of defaulted student borrowers also were never told about the massive penalties and fees that would be attached to their loans if they defaulted; they had to find out the hard way, after it was too late. No mention was ever made to them that their professional licenses could be suspended and their income tax returns, wages, and Social Security income could be seized as a result of their defaulting on their student loans.

Until consumer protections are restored to education loans, and until Congress puts an end to the ruthless collection tactics employed by the student loan collection industry, students are well advised to educate themselves about these facts. In most instances, entrance loan counseling does not cover these topics in sufficient detail, and they are often set up on Web sites, which minimizes the effectiveness of the information transmission. (Some counseling sites are even implemented by the lenders, who have a vested interest in maximizing their revenues, not minimizing student debt.) In other words, the student can easily pass through the counseling session without actually learning anything.

Students need to be aware of the unique and harsh consequences of defaulting on student loans. It is only in this way that they can make well-informed decisions about whether—and from where—to obtain loans for college.

Graduation: To Consolidate or Not

Graduating from college or leaving school for other reasons represents a critical juncture with regard to student loans. It is here that the most students consider whether or not to consolidate their loans, which means bundling loans into a single loan with a new (or the same) lender. The interest rate for consolidation loans is the weighted average of the original loans rounded up to the nearest eighth of a percent. For federally guaranteed loans (such as Stafford, PLUS, and so forth), consolidating loans is allowed only once; therefore, after a student consolidates, he or she is stuck with that lender for the life of the loan. Of course, if a borrower takes out an additional loan, consolidation can occur again, but it is not advisable to take out a student loan for the sole purpose of consolidation, although perhaps leaving a small loan out of the consolidation would be a prudent action to take to preserve the option of refinancing later.

For federal loans, companies often offer some discounts for consolidation, such as interest rate reductions for on-time payments and automatic withdrawals, but only a minority of borrowers actually receive these benefits throughout the life of the loan. For one reason or another (for example, a missed payment or a late payment), these benefits are taken away from perhaps 90 percent of borrowers. In fact, most borrowers who lose prompt payment discounts do so on the very first payment.

Also, consolidation of loans often results in the loans being changed from subsidized to unsubsidized. This can have a significant effect on the borrower if a deferment is required in times of unemployment or other periods of financial distress, since the government pays the interest on the subsidized portion of the loan during deferment (but not forbearance). Borrowers should prefer deferments over forbearances and try to pay at least the interest during a forbearance to keep the loan balance from growing.

It cannot be emphasized enough that under current federal law, consolidation of student loans represents the last opportunity the student will have to shop his or her loans around to find the best terms. Until federal law opens up the marketplace to more competition and provides borrowers with the freedom to refinance the debt, borrowers must do as much research as possible on this prior to consolidation so they are able to make informed decisions based on the range of possible scenarios that might befall them. Web sites like FinAid.org provide current information about borrower discounts available for student consolidation loans. FinAid.org also provides a wide array of cost and repayment calculators that the borrower would do well to try before making any final decisions about loans.

Loan Forgiveness for Public Service

For people who have a large amount of debt and who plan on entering public service after graduation, a new program passed into law with the College Cost Reduction and Access Act of 2007 may be the only way to pay off student loan debts in a reasonable amount of time. It is the public service loan forgiveness program, and it forgives the remaining balance of Direct Loans after 120 payments are made. There is a requirement, however: borrowers must be employed full-time in a public service job while re-paying the debt. This includes working for federal, state, or local government, 501c(3) nonprofit organizations, law enforcement, and other positions as defined by the new legislation.

This program is very attractive for new graduates who have high debt loads and career aspirations in the public sector. How-ever, the borrower must have a loan through the Direct Loan Program, which means that FFELP borrowers have to consoli-date their loans into this program. The program is also attractive in that an income-based repayment plan or income-sensitive contingent repayment plan can be used throughout the term. It does have its risks also, though. For example, under current law, the amount that is forgiven at the end of the ten-year term is counted as taxable income. This could be a very large amount, depending upon the original debt load of the borrower and his or her income during the repayment period. Here is another risk: borrowers who decide after a few years of repayment that public service isn't for them may be worse off than when they started, since any unpaid interest is capitalized.

For defaulted borrowers whose debt loads have already sky-rocketed and whose earnings are low, this taxable event could prove to be devastating. Other problems exist with the service forgiveness program from the perspective of longtime defaulted borrowers and are described in the previous chapter. For de-faulted borrowers in this circumstance, unfortunately, there sim-ply are no workable options under the current law that would allow the debt to be satisfied in a reasonable amount of time.

Financial Problems During Repayment, and Options

At one point or another during loan repayment, many if not most borrowers will face periods of unemployment and other financial difficulties that limit their ability to make their sched-uled loan payments. Congress mandates that forbearances or de-ferments be made available to the borrowers during these times.

These options must be applied for, and Congress gives lenders a wide range of authority for approving or denying these applications. If the loan is subsidized, the government will cover interest on the loans during deferment. Otherwise, interest will continue to accrue on these loans, and at the end of the deferment or forbearance term, the borrower will owe even more. Note also that using a forbearance or deferment will almost certainly end whatever borrower benefits were enjoyed up to that point.

As has been shown throughout this book, there can be a perverse incentive for a lender to make borrowers default on their loans, particularly if that lender also owns or controls guarantor or collection agencies, as Sallie Mae does. There is much well-documented evidence of lenders making false claims to the federal government in order to receive payment on defaulted loans (see chapter 3). It is for this reason that borrowers are urged very strongly to keep detailed records of their applications for deferment and forbearance, as well as complete records of when each payment was made. Borrowers should send requests for forbearance by certified mail, return receipt requested, or by FedEx or another overnight carrier so that they have formal records of when the requests were received and by whom. A paper trail is very important, particularly since under current law, once a loan is defaulted, there is little or no recourse for the borrower. There is no appeals process for defaulted loans. Lenders are notorious for losing paperwork or claiming to have received it late. Once a guaranty agency pays a claim on a defaulted loan, they keep track of the payment history only from that point onward, and they consider the loan balance to be legitimate.

"I sent my deferment request in the first time; they said they never received it." "Dealing with the lender on my deferment was like trying to push a wet noodle upstairs with a chopstick." "They didn't even mention that I could ask for a forbearance."

"Every time I called to check on my deferment, I would get nowhere." Problems occurring during the deferment and forbearance application process are a primary way that loans are led into default. Many, many stories have been received from borrowers whose only mistakes were not following up on their deferment or forbearance requests with the lenders. Until the lender notifies you that the deferment or forbearance has been granted, you should continue making payments on your loans.

Also, in light of the various False Claims Act violations that were described earlier in this book, borrowers who know that they are in repayment but who are not receiving invoices or statements by mail from the lenders should be wary; do not for a moment make the mistake of thinking that just because the lender is not billing you, you are under no legal obligation to pay. You still have to make the payments even if you receive no mail from the lender. Contacting the lender at this point is the best advice. Make sure the lender has your current contact information at all times.

According to Jennifer, a mother in Georgia, such an oversight can cost a borrower dearly. Unemployed in 2006, Jennifer applied for an economic-hardship deferment. She never received anything from her lender, nothing saying that the application had been either approved or denied. She says she did receive a six-month statement in June 2007 showing that interest had accrued on the account, but there was no demand for payment, and she was never otherwise contacted by her lender. It was only when she attempted to consolidate her loans under one lender (she had student debt from both undergraduate and graduate school) that she was told that the loans for which she believed she was in deferment had been put into default. She went through the standard painful attempts at negotiating with various entities who "tossed her loan around, adding fees and interest the whole way." To date, she faces wage garnishment and is completely lost about what to do now. She fears for both her and her daughter's welfare.

If you are married and file a joint income tax return, use the innocent-spouse defense to fight lender attempts to attach income tax refunds. Part of the income tax refund belongs to the spouse who didn't default on his or her debts, and the lender has no right to that money.

Loan Cancellation

There are at least some provisions in federal law for the cancellation of federally guaranteed student loan debt, and it is important for the borrowers to be aware of this. A provision applies if the borrower becomes totally and permanently disabled. This requires an approved doctor's certification of the total and permanent disability. Often, the loan holder will use his or her own doctor to provide a second opinion, and this is the cause of frequent disputes. Disability discharge is rarely granted, since the "total and permanent" caveat means exactly that. A short-term disability is insufficient. Many borrowers who have been granted disability benefits are rudely surprised when they find that their disability income is being garnished.

There is also a provision for loan cancellation under the "ability to benefit" clause. Examples of this given by the U.S. Department of Education include a school admitting a student who did not satisfy the application requirements for ability to benefit from the training, such as if the student did not possess a high school diploma or GED and had not taken an ATB test. Another example is if a school signed the student's name without that student's authorization on the loan application or promissory note. This provision also allows cancellation if the borrower had a physical, mental, or legal status or condition at the time of enrollment that would legally bar employment in their field of study. Finally, this provision provides for loan cancellation if the student was the victim of identity theft.

School closure is also an important and legitimate basis for loan cancellation. The students attending the Silver State Helicopter school, for example, would have been granted loan cancellation had their loans been federally guaranteed. One note of caution here: schools that close will often graduate students just prior to closing so that they are able to say that they fulfilled their duty to the student. This is a frequent basis for complaints at the StudentLoanJustice.org Web site.

One such student is Don Gilbert, the typesetter mentioned in chapter 3 whose school closed in January 2001 while he was still enrolled. Don filled out the necessary forms to qualify for loan cancellation but was nonetheless pursued by loan collectors. According to Don, the loan holder refuses to acknowledge that the school closed while Don was still enrolled, and despite his complaints to the state attorney general, the Department of Education, and others, he is unable to close this account. He is frustrated beyond belief.

One Novel Approach for Avoiding Default

If a borrower is unable to work with a loan holder to convince the company to approve the deferment or forbearance application, there is one method for ensuring that the loan does not default. According to the Higher Education Act of 1965 (HEA), a loan is not considered to be in default unless no payment has been made on the loan for 270 days. Thus, if a borrower makes any payment—even for an insignificant amount—on the loan at least every 269 days, then legally the loan cannot be in default. While this method can and does indeed work, as borrowers have reported, it does not prevent interest from accruing on the loan, and it does not prevent other fees (for example, late fees) from being attached to the debt. However, borrowers should be aware of this information, and in the event that a loan is bordering on default and the lender refuses to grant the deferments or forbearance that is required, a nominal payment—sent by registered mail—may be the only option to avoid default.

Defaulted Loans

As this book clearly demonstrates, the negative consequences of a defaulted loan, particularly if the amounts involved are large, are serious, debilitating, and often lead to massive problems for the borrower well beyond his or her credit record and job security. Moreover, the programs available for satisfying this debt, such as loan rehabilitation, are problematic at best. In all cases of defaulted loans, the borrower can rest assured that while the loan holder was perhaps less than engaged in contacting the borrower prior to default, the collection companies will more than make up for this lack of effort after the loan has defaulted. Harassing collection calls of more than ten times per day have been reported, and egregious violations of the Fair Debt Collection and Practices Act (FDCPA) have been reported many times. Some of these are detailed in chapter 3.

Despite the fact that nonprofit loan agencies are exempted from coverage under the FDCPA, the borrower should be aware that for-profit collection companies—even if they are collecting on behalf of an exempt agency—are still bound by this act. Some violations of this act are described below.[4]

Harassing and/or Abusive Statements:

- Threatening to have you arrested or jailed
- Threatening to take your SSI or other protected income
- Threatening to take your household furniture
- Threatening to cause physical injury to you or your property
- Threatening members of your family

- Threatening to send false information about you to the credit reporting agencies
- Using obscene or profane language

False and/or Misleading Statements:

- Misrepresenting the character, amount, or legal status of the debt
- Making empty threats to scare you
- Pretending to work for a credit reporting agency
- Pretending to work for a government agency
- Falsely claiming to be an attorney or to work with attorneys
- Sending fake legal papers to confuse you, or telling you to ignore real legal papers

Abusive and/or Unfair Practices:

- Calling you or any other person repeatedly with intent to annoy, harass, or abuse
- Calling you after you have sent a cease letter
- Calling or contacting you without disclosing that they are debt collectors trying to collect a debt
- Collecting interest, fees, collection expenses, or other charges that are not authorized by your original payment agreement
- Soliciting postdated checks with the intent to threaten to expose you to criminal charges, or soliciting postdated checks and then threatening to deposit them early
- Contacting you by postcard, or contacting you in any way that would disclose to a third party that they are debt collectors

Of these violations, a few are commonly reported by student loan borrowers. These include collectors claiming to be with the

Department of Education; collection companies attempting to initiate rehabilitation; collectors attaching unannounced fees to the debt; and collectors discussing the borrower's financial situation with family members and coworkers, particularly after being specifically told not to call the borrower at work.

Borrowers who are being hounded by collection companies need to be aware of these potential violations and document them if necessary. All defaulted borrowers interested in protecting their rights should consider acquiring phone recording equipment, which is relatively inexpensive. This is, of course, most effective in states where recorded evidence is admissible in a court of law. If the borrower does not live in a state in which phone recordings are admissible in court, then the borrower does need to announce that the call may be recorded. There are subtle methods for making this announcement that are left to the reader to determine. If none of this is possible, then, at the very least, borrowers should keep an active log of phone calls, notations regarding what was said, and the names that the callers used to identify themselves. For further information about specific collection company activities that are violations of the FDCPA, the reader is advised to visit the Better Business Bureau (http://welcome.bbb.org), the National Consumer Law Center (www.nclc.org), and other resources.

Avoid Dealing with Guarantors and Third-Party Collection Companies

There are many middlemen associated with defaulted federal student loans. First, there is the lender who originates the loan. Then there is the guarantor who (supposedly) guarantees the loan against default. Next there are collection companies that the guarantor uses to collect on the defaulted loan. Finally, there is the U.S. Department of Education (or the Department of Health and Human Services for HEAL loans), the organizations that actually provide the guaranty for the loan when it defaults.

All of these entities combine to present a confusing, intimidating, and, ultimately, expensive front that the borrower must contend with.

Most defaulted borrowers resign themselves to dealing with the guarantors and their collection companies. Regardless of the circumstances of default, there is typically no negotiating with the guarantor or the collection company. The borrower is forced, through rehabilitation, wage garnishment, or other mechanisms, to ultimately repay a much larger amount than the originally defaulted loan. Borrowers can and do exert significant time and effort attempting to deal with ombudsmen who work for the guarantors, and this effort is almost always wasted.

If a borrower is unwilling or unable to comply with the demands put upon him by the guarantor, there is another option that is used occasionally. The borrower can demand that the loans be transferred directly to the true guarantor of the loan, the U.S. Department of Education. By making this demand, the borrower can at least get the loan out of the hands of the state guarantor agency and perhaps be able to negotiate a more favorable outcome.

This is admittedly an unproven piece of advice. However, rationally, it seems that dealing directly with the ultimate backer of the loan probably holds more promise than attempting to negotiate with middleman agencies who have no incentive or desire to negotiate (despite their status as nonprofit agencies with a public benefit charter).

Political winds can and do change over time, and this may help defaulted borrowers. With a new president and Congress, one must hope that there will be significant staffing and other changes within the U.S. Department of Education that will lead to more favorable treatment for defaulted borrowers. Certainly, it couldn't be any worse, given the infuriating unwillingness of the U.S. Department of Education to acknowledge the real harm that its policies have caused the public over the past decade.

Bankruptcy

While it is extremely difficult to discharge student loan debt in bankruptcy proceedings, there are circumstances under which it can be done. In general, the bankruptcy courts use a three-prong test to determine whether a student loan debt is eligible for discharge. One test is the answer to this question: Would the borrower be able to maintain a minimal standard of living if forced to repay the loan? This test often uses the monthly payments that would be made under the income-contingent repayment program. The second test requires that there be evidence that the hardship is likely to continue for a significant portion of the loan-repayment period. The third test is whether or not the borrower made good-faith efforts to repay the loan before he or she filed for bankruptcy (usually this means that the borrower has been in repayment for some time).

For most borrowers who have at least basic means, such as the ability to work, student loan debt is not dischargeable in bankruptcy. However, there are a few slim opportunities. One important factor is that it is left to the judge to interpret this three-prong test, and so, depending on the judge, there may be some flexibility in the ability of the debtor to discharge this debt in bankruptcy proceedings. As time goes on and as it becomes apparent to the general public how harmful the bankruptcy laws are for student loan debtors, there may be some expansion of these rights. Judges can and hopefully will realize this and act in a more forgiving manner in the future. Of course, this depends on how active the citizens who are faced with this unique type of debt load become, and how successful they are.

One judge who has been noticed in the community is Joel B. Rosenthal, a U.S. Bankruptcy Court judge in Massachusetts who challenged the notion that the Direct Loan forgiveness program could be considered a substitute for bankruptcy protections. In a legal proceeding, he stated:

There are several problems with this program, including that the forgiveness of debt outside of bankruptcy results in a taxable event and that Social Security payments can be garnished to pay down these taxes. Such a program removes from this Court's consideration the very issue Congress entrusted to the Court, namely the repayment of the debt would impose an undue hardship. To hold that debtors must participate in the Ford program, if eligible, would be no more than the Court abdicating its responsibility to determine the dischargeability of a student loan. If this is the outcome Congress intended, it would have said so.[5]

So there is reason to be hopeful that until such time as bankruptcy protections are returned to student loans and they are treated like any other type of unsecured debt, some judges may be willing to give the benefit of the doubt to the consumers rather than to the banks with regards to issues of bankruptcy.

Portions of Private Loans May Be Dischargeable in Bankruptcy

As a practical matter, people who obtained private loans well beyond their means to repay should realize that under the new federal bankruptcy code, although private loans were reclassified and are treated in the same manner as federally guaranteed loans, there is a caveat: As defined by the new legislation, the portion of the private loan that is largely exempt from bankruptcy protections is only that portion that was used to pay for the cost of attendance at the university. This includes tuition, room and board, and school supplies such as books, papers, and other expenses directly related to attending college. Other expenses do not qualify by the IRS definition, and thus cannot be considered a "qualified education loan." In layman's terms: If you took out a private loan and used the money for anything other than the cost of attendance of the college, then by law, this amount should be treated like any other type of debt for the purposes of inclusion in bankruptcy proceedings and be fully dischargeable according to current bankruptcy laws.[6]

Contact Members of Congress

While this sounds like boilerplate advice, in fact, it is not. Congressional and senatorial offices have a duty to serve their constituents. There are two compelling reasons why borrowers in distress about their student loans should contact their local elected representatives. First, there may be some valuable assistance these offices can provide for the individual borrowers in their attempts to come to a fair and reasonable outcome for their loans. While as best as can be determined this does not happen with any great frequency, there is at least a chance that the offices can provide some recourse.

More important, however, borrowers should contact their local officials because these representatives need to understand the depth, breadth, and seriousness of the student loan problem. Only by hearing from constituents can these legislators learn about the injustices that are occurring and take action to address them. Student loan borrowers, particularly those whose debt has exploded to unmanageable proportions, need to realize that suffering in silence serves only to perpetuate a predatory lending system that is in critical need of reform.

Become Publicly Active

Defaulted borrowers who do not earn enough to satisfy the overwhelming burden of their escalated student loan debt have, under current law, nowhere to turn. It therefore is incumbent upon them to take it upon themselves to bring this issue to the public eye. Borrowers are encouraged first to educate themselves about the overall problem, and then to act to solve it.

Beyond making calls to elected officials, there are a number of simple, inexpensive activities that borrowers can undertake to bring needed attention to this issue and inspire the necessary political will to restore consumer protections to student loans. A good first step is to go to the StudentLoanJustice.org Web site and tell your story for the record. You can then meet others in your state who are facing similar difficulties, and proceed from there. There are flyers and brochures at the site that can be downloaded, printed, and posted in public areas. Of course, SLJ has no monopoly on the grassroots effort to restore standard consumer protections to student loans, and borrowers are strongly encouraged to act independently as their skills permit to help solve this problem.

For example, anyone can start his or her own Web site or blog that both tells one's own personal story and speaks to the larger issues. While this may seem emotionally difficult to do—after all, no one wants to talk publicly about personal financial situations—it is an important step to take in order to bring about legislative solutions to the problem. Dozens of people have already begun to do this, and it is already paying significant dividends, although there is much more to accomplish.

Another easy step is to convince local and national reporters to cover this issue from the borrower's perspective. There is no shortage of compelling stories out there to tell, and most reporters, when they study the problem at any length, will arrive at the same conclusion: namely, that there is a problem, and something needs to be done about it. Borrowers are advised to pay attention to which reporters in their local areas might be most appropriate for such a story, and then act accordingly to give the reporter everything needed to generate a story that describes the problem.

As mentioned before, the media is extremely important for communicating the nature and depth of the student loan problem. The media includes not only newspapers but also radio, television, the Internet, and other outlets. Borrowers who decide to take up the challenge of citizen activism are encouraged to use all of these avenues to communicate the problem to the general public.

In general, it is advisable not to go over the top when discussing this issue in public, despite your heartfelt indignation. Doing so only galvanizes support for those who would prefer that student loans remain without consumer protections. The argument for the return of standard consumer protections for student loans is a strong and convincing one, and inserting too much emotion into it not only does not help move the argument forward, it actually hinders progress. I can attest to this personally, after having pushed the Send button too soon on a number of occasions. And of course, use nonviolent means only. To do otherwise would most assuredly have the opposite effect from what is desired.

By way of encouragement: it was only because citizen activists lobbied Congress and influenced media stories that the Student Borrower Bill of Rights was created.[7] Citizen activists also were featured prominently by Senator Durbin when he rolled out legislation that would have restored bankruptcy protections for private student loans. The public consciousness on the student loan issue has changed dramatically in the past two to three years, so future citizen efforts should meet with less resistance and more acceptance as time goes on.

Epilogue

After I'd finished writing this book, a number of important events transpired in the student loan industry that effectively shifted the public debate farther away from the critical need to restore standard consumer protections for student loans. It is likely that these events and the ensuing public discourse and legislative action will only exacerbate the stresses being felt by student loan borrowers caught in the student loan scam and make the need for consumer protections all the more critical. Without question, recent events significantly bolstered the arguments made in this book.

Also, the U.S. economy is headed for recession. The paralysis that gripped the home mortgage industry reverberated in the student loan sector. Indeed, the secondary market for both federally guaranteed and private loans seized up in spring 2007. Lenders' inability to sell their bundled loans to investors was cause for serious concern. Also, defaults on private loans increased significantly—despite borrowers' awareness that they no longer had bankruptcy protection. In light of this credit crisis, stock prices across the student loan sector fell, and fell abruptly. In a one-month period in late 2007, Sallie Mae's stock dropped by more than half, prompting margin calls against the holdings of its CEO, Albert Lord, who, at the end of a tumultuous conference call with investors was heard saying "Let's get the fuck out of here."

Simultaneously, some lending companies, incensed by recent congressional action that made their loans less profitable, began announcing that they would be withdrawing from making certain types of loans. College Loan Corporation (CLC), for instance, announced in February that it would no longer participate in the Federal Family Education Loan (FFEL) Program as a result of congressional action that cut into the subsidies on loans that lenders receive from the federal government. CEO Carey Katz said that the changes in the program made it unattractive for mid-sized student loan companies like CLC to be in the business.

The threat of banks withdrawing from the FFEL program snapped Congress to attention. By May 7, President Bush had signed into law emergency legislation that designated the U.S. Department of Education a lender of last resort, authorizing the department to purchase bundled loans from lenders. The legislation also increased by $2,000 the loan limits for students borrowing through the Stafford loan program.

The speed with which Congress acted to accommodate the lending industry, in contrast to the glacial congressional response to calls for the return of consumer protections, is very telling. The needs of the borrowers—particularly those facing severe financial hardship—has been moved another notch downward on the list of congressional priorities regarding student loans.

Equally disturbing are the remarks of Albert Lord, who ended a recent conference call with jittery investors by reassuring them that federally guaranteed student loans are still "recession proof," meaning that the perverse machinations by which lenders/guarantors make far more money when students default are still intact. Sallie Mae's earnings will almost certainly accelerate when defaults increase in the near future. The arguments in this book will undoubtedly be even more relevant and urgent in time.

Finally, I feel it is important to note the following: Chapter 3 details the statements made by a current employee of the Kentucky Higher Education Assistance Authority (KHEAA). This employee tells of a nonprofit that has spun out of control—one that was marketing loans to disadvantaged populations in the knowledge that these borrowers would likely default on their loans and thus make the company more revenue through wage, Social Security, and other garnishments. I received word on May 14, 2007, from a neutral third party, that this employee had been suspended from his job—ostensibly because he was "mentally unfit." In my opinion, and in the opinion of the person who gave me this news—a noted reporter—this employee was in no way mentally unfit or unstable. Rather, he struck us both as being angry and tired of participating in activities that he knew were hurting rather than helping those who the KHEAA was supposed to be serving. He's a true whistleblower, in my opinion.

I can't help but think that our email exchanges—many of which he sent directly from his company email account—may have been intercepted, and that his suspension was a preemptive attempt by KHEAA to discredit him. I can only hope that he will be vindicated, and that the truth about the organization will come out.

Acknowledgments

I would like to acknowledge Catherine Tumber, currently with the *Boston Review* and formerly with the *Boston Phoenix*, for her early dedication as a journalist to this issue, and also for the advice and guidance that made this book possible. I would like to thank my editor, Gayatri Patnaik, for her enthusiasm for and dedication to this project. I would also like to acknowledge the legislative work performed by Senators Ted Kennedy, Hillary Clinton, and Dick Durbin, and Congressmen George Miller and Danny Davis. Their work has given student borrowers reason to have some hope for the future. Finally, I want to acknowledge the courage of the borrowers who have allowed their stories to be used for this work.

The following people and resources were very useful during the research for this book:

Deanne Loonin and Gary Klein of the National Consumer Law Center (NCLC.org) and their book *Surviving Debt: A Guide for Consumers in Financial Stress*

Bob Shireman of the Institute for College Access and Success (Ticas.org)

Stephen Burd and Michael Dannenberg of the New America Foundation (NewAmerica.Net)

Appendix

Sallie Mae Stock Set Aside for Employees[1]

Year	Stock Set Aside for Employees	2nd filing	3rd filing	Total	Employees (estimate)	Average per Employee
2005	$107,647,800			$107,647,800	8000	$13,456
2004	$575,100,000			$575,100,000	7200	$79,875
2003	$233,490,000	$85,000,000		$318,490,000	6800	$46,837
2002	$1,718,465,296			$1,718,465,296	6300	$272,772
2001	$50,000,000	$31,839,116	$18,160,917	$100,000,033	5700	$17,544
2000				$0	5100	$0
1999	$25,000,000			$25,000,000	4500	$5,556
1998	$241,312,500	$432,091,800		$673,404,300	4000	$168,351
1997	$86,718,234	$35,156,250		$121,874,484	3500	$34,821
			TOTALS	$3,639,981,913		$639,212

$50 million was set aside for "Key USA Group Employees" following the buyout

EdFund Executive Salaries Since 1999[2]

	2003	2002	2001	2000	1999
Becky Stilling	$263,523	$251,504	$214,506	$211,144	$127,815
Rothman (VP finance)	$246,233	$226,795	$179,036	$157,964	$99,876
Wendie Doyle (counsel)	$225,717	$215,937	$163,854	$36,532	—
Dorene Hoops		$174,954	$54,146	—	—
William Ramsey		$216,497	$166,464	$143,690	$101,327
Theresa Bickler		$204,760	$184,692	$170,653	$114,456
Callihan		$211,127	$193,811	$175,813	$119,062
Damskey		$147,183	$99,991	—	—
Ninemire		$197,918	$110,881	—	—

Notes

Chapter One: The Rise of Sallie Mae and the Fall of Consumer Protections

1. Wyatt Kingseed, "The 'Bonus Army' War in Washington," www.historynet.com.
2. Lyndon Baines Johnson Presidential Library and Museum, www.lbjlib.utexas.edu/johnson/lbjforkids/edu_timeline.shtm.
3. Ibid.
4. U.S. Bureau of the Census, "Population Characteristics: Educational Attainment," December 1962 and March 1970.
5. Ibid.
6. Ibid.
7. U.S. Census Bureau online report: www.census.gov/prod/2002pubs/01statab/educ.pdf.
8. Ralph Nader, "The Student Business" http://nader.org, May 9, 2006.
9. Sallie Mae annual reports, 2003–2005.
10. Ibid.
11. Sallie Mae S-8 filings, 1997–2005.
12. Bethany McLean, "When Sallie Met Wall Street," *Fortune,* December 26, 2005.
13. John Hechinger, "U.S. Gets Tough on Failure to Repay Student Loans," *Wall Street Journal,* January 6, 2004.
14. Larry L. Leslie and Gary P. Johnson, "The Market Model and Higher Education," *The Journal of Higher Education* 45, no. 1 (January 1974): 1–20.
15. Ibid.
16. Dr. Larry Leslie, e-mail message to the author, October 5, 2007.
17. "Changes Sought at Student Loan Marketing Association," *Chronicle of Higher Education,* April 21, 1995.
18. Megan Barnett and Julian Barnes, "Big Money on Campus," *U.S. News & World Report,* October 27, 2003.
19. Ibid.
20. Steve Koff, "Boehner in Line to Be House Majority Leader," *Cleveland Plain Dealer,* January 10, 2006.

21. "The Student Business," Ralph Nader, http://nader.org, May 9, 2006.

22. Estimate provided by Mark Kantrowitz, publisher, www.FinAid.org.

23. U.S. Bureau of the Census, "Population Characteristics: Educational Attainment," December 1962 and March 1970.

24. Kevin Bruns, "Counterpoint: Lenders Respond," *Inside Higher Ed,* October 20, 2006.

25. B. Hennessy, "The Partial Discharge of Student Loans: Breaking Apart the All or Nothing Interpretation of 11 U.S.C. 523 (A)(8)," *Temple Law Review* 71 (2004). See http://strategis.ic.gc.ca/epic/site/bsf-osb.nsf/en/br01679e.html.

26. These sentiments regarding the overwhelming power of the student loan lobbying forces on Capitol Hill are held by many noted experts, including Professor Elizabeth Warren (Harvard University), Stephen Burd and Michael Dannenberg (New America Foundation), and Bob Shireman (Institute for College Access and Success).

27. Although nonprofit, state-run guarantors were exempt from this act, for-profit collection companies that they contract with do have to adhere to it. This is seen as one of the few pieces of legislation that borrowers can use to protect themselves from the industry. The application of this act to student loans is described more fully in chapter 9.

28. Sallie Mae annual report, 2003.

29. Sallie Mae, "Sallie Mae Posts Strong Third-Quarter 2006 Performance Results," press release, October 19, 2006.

Chapter Two: Who Benefited

1. Erin Dillon, "Leading Lady: Sallie Mae and the Origins of Today's Student Loan Controversy," *Education Sector Report,* May 2007.

2. Sallie Mae, annual report, 2005.

3. Ibid.

4. Andrew Sorkin, "The Money Game and the Mind Game at Sallie Mae," *New York Times,* October 7, 2007.

5. Bethany McLean, "Sallie Mae: A Hot Stock, a Tough Lender," *Fortune* magazine, December 26, 2005.

6. Thomas Heath, "Lord Is Willing to Toot His Horn," *Washington Post,* November 5, 2005.

7. Bob Shireman, "How Non-Profit Student Loan Officials Get Rich," TICAS briefing paper, May 26, 2005.

8. EdFund IRS 990 filings, 1998–2003.

9. Sorkin, "The Money Game."

10. E-mail from StudentLoanJustice.org members to House and Senate Education Committee staff, July 26, 2007.

11. Bethany McLean, "Back to School," *Fortune* magazine, November 27, 2006.

12. Marcus Katz, interview with author, December 10, 2006.

13. Robert Reich, "The Real Scandal of Student Loans," Robert Reich's Blog, April 2007, http://robertreich.blogspot.com/ 2007_04_01_archive.html.

14. Office of the Inspector General, "Review of Financial Partners' Monitoring and Oversight of Guaranty Agencies, Lenders, and Servicers," Office of the Inspector General final audit report, September 2006.

Chapter Three: Collection Abuses

1. Lesley Stahl, "Sallie Mae's Success Too Costly?" *60 Minutes,* May 7, 2006.

2. Office of the Inspector General, "Sallie Mae Pays $3.4 Million to Settle Civil False Claims Act Allegations," press release, January 5, 2001.

3. Jeff Selingo, "Student Loan Collection Company Pleads Guilty in Student Loan Fraud Case," *Chronicle of Higher Education,* May 22, 1998.

4. Office of the Inspector General, "U.S. Settles Suit Against Corus Bank for Student Loan Fraud," press release, April 7, 2000.

5. Sallie Mae, Annual 10-K Filing 2006, www.salliemae.com/about/ investors/stockholderinfo/secfilings/secfilings.htm.

6. See their Web site, premierecredit.com/whysharks.cfm.

7. David Hilzenrath, "Kennedy Targets Sallie Mae's Role," *Washington Post,* November 17, 2006.

8. U.S. Senate, "Kennedy Questions Student Loan Lenders' Collection Tactics," press release, April 26, 2007.

9. National Center for Education Statistics, "Dealing with Debt: 1992–93 Bachelor's Degree Recipients Ten Years Later," June 2006.

10. Erin Dillon, "Hidden Details: A Closer Look at Student Loan Default Rates," *Education Sector,* October 23, 2007.

11. Scott Jaschik and Doug Lederman, "Damning Data on Defaults," *Inside Higher Ed,* December 4, 2007.

Chapter Four: The Borrowers

1. Dave Newbart, "Man Commits Suicide—Burdened by Student Loans," *Chicago Sun-Times,* September 24, 2007.

Chapter Five: The Oversight Fiasco

1. John Hechinger and Anne-Marie Chaker, "Did Revolving Door Lead to Student Loan Mess? Critics Blame Lax Oversight Resulting from Close Ties of Industry, Government," *Wall Street Journal,* April 13, 2007.

2. Office of the Inspector General, "Review of Financial Partners' Monitoring and Oversight of Guaranty Agencies, Lenders, and Servicers, Final Audit Report," U.S. Department of Education, ED-OIG/A04E0009, September 2006.

3. Sam Dillon, "Spellings Rejects Criticism on Student Loan Scandal," *New York Times,* May 11, 2007.

4. Megan Barnett and Julian Barnes, "Big Money on Campus," *U.S. News & World Report,* October 19, 2003.

5. Ibid.

6. Ibid.

7. Estimate provided by Mark Kantrowitz, www.FinAid.org.

8. Lesley Stahl, "Sallie Mae's Success Too Costly?" *60 Minutes,* May 7, 2006.

9. Stephen Burd, "Report Backed by Student Loan Industry Challenges the Notion that Direct Lending Saves Money," *Chronicle of Higher Education,* March 3, 2005.

10. Office of the Inspector General, "Review of Financial Partners' Monitoring and Oversight."

11. Ibid.

12. Ibid.

13. Ibid.

14. Office of the Inspector General, "Special Allowance Payments to Nelnet for Loans funded by Tax-Exempt Obligations," U.S. Department of Education, September 2006.

15. Ibid.

16. Amit Paley, "Confusion Cited in Overpayments to Student Lenders," *Washington Post,* October 20, 2007.

17. Spreadsheet provided by Mr. Jon Oberg, retired Department of Education analyst, on October 18, 2007.

18. Stahl, "Sallie Mae's Success Too Costly?"

19. Ibid.

20. Mirek Halaska, Department of Education analyst, e-mail to department officials, July 14, 2004.

21. Senator Ted Kennedy, "Senator Kennedy Leads Congress in Crackdown on Student Loan Scandal," press release, October 9, 2004.

22. Ibid.

23. Stahl, "Sallie Mae's Success Too Costly?"

24. U.S. Department of Education, press release, June 11, 2002.

25. Jonathan Glater, "U.S. Ignores Findings on Student Lender," *New York Times,* January 26, 2008. --

26. Ibid.

27. Senator Ted Kennedy, press release, April 12, 2007.

28. Ibid.

29. Paul Basken, "As Investigations of Student-Loan Providers Reach Education Dept., Lenders Defend Practices," *Chronicle of Higher Education,* April 6, 2007.

30. Ana Alaya, "New Jersey Student Loan Agency Got Kickbacks from Sallie Mae," *Newark Star-Ledger,* May 1, 2007.

31. Ibid.

32. Ibid.

33. Paul Basken, "Critics Question Sallie Mae's Close Ties with Agency that Guarantees Its Loans," *Chronicle of Higher Education,* May 4, 2007.

34. Paul Basken, "Suspended Department of Education Official Had Approved 2004 Conflict Waiver for Former Employer, Sallie Mae." See http://chronicle.com/weekly/v53/i37/37a01801.htm.

35. Robert Shireman, "A Questionable Arrangement," HigherEdWatch.org, May 31, 2007.

36. Senator Paul Simon, letter to the Internal Revenue Service, July 18, 1996.

Chapter Six: The Corruption of the Universities

1. Lesley Stahl, "Sallie Mae's Success Too Costly?" *60 Minutes,* May 7, 2006.

2. These findings are excerpted from Attorney General Cuomo's press release dated March 15, 2007.

3. New York State Attorney General's Office, press release, July 20, 2007.

4. Robert Siegel, interview with attorney general Andrew Cuomo, National Public Radio, June 8, 2007.

5. U.S. Senate Committee on Health, Education, Labor, and Pensions, "Report on Marketing Practices in the Federal Family Education Loan Program," June 14, 2007.

6. Ibid.

7. Kevin Zelaya, "N.Y. Official Studies Dealings of University, Lenders," *Daily Nebraskan,* February 15, 2007.

8. Stephen Burd, "News Scoop: Stock Options Provided to Financial Aid Officials by Student Loan Provider," *Higher Ed Watch,* April 4, 2007.

9. Geoff Larcom, "EMU Sends Back Donor Money," *Ann Arbor News,* August 11, 2007.

10. New York State Attorney General's Office, press release, December 11, 2007.

11. Ibid.

12. Mr. Dallas A. Martin, supplemental statement to the U.S. House of Representatives, May 12, 2004.

13. Paul Basken, "Education Department Seeks More Information from Fifty-five Colleges on Dealings with Student Lenders," *Chronicle of Higher Education,* November 27, 2007.

14. Doug Lederman, "Education Department, on the Case," *Inside Higher Ed,* July 10, 2007.

Chapter Seven: The Grass Roots Awaken

1. John A. E. Pottow, "The Nondischargeability of Student Loans in Personal Bankruptcy Proceedings: The Search for a Theory," *Canadian Business Law Journal* 44 (March 2007): 245–78.

2. Ibid.

3. Bethany McLean, "Sallie Mae: A Hot Stock, a Tough Lender," *Fortune* magazine, December 26, 2005.

4. Anya Kamenetz, "Your Late Fees, Their Millions," *Village Voice,* January 17, 2006.

5. Lesley Stahl, "Sallie Mae's Success Too Costly?" *60 Minutes,* May 7, 2006.

6. Dr. Gregory Walton, Office of Senator Hillary Clinton, e-mail to SLJ, May 26, 2006.

7. Dave Newbart, "Law Favors Gambler over Grad," *Chicago Sun-Times,* May 6, 2007.

8. Elizabeth Redden, "More than a Rabble Rouser?" *Inside Higher Ed,* January 12, 2007.

9. Catherine Tumber, "Manhandled No More," *Boston Phoenix,* December 14, 2006.

10. Scott Jaschik and Doug Lederman, "Damning Data on Defaults," *Inside Higher Ed,* December 4, 2007.

11. Erin Dillon, "Hidden Details: A Closer Look at Student Loan Default Rates," *Education Sector,* October 23, 2007.

12. Marcy Gordon, "Sallie Mae Lost $1.6 Billion in 4Q," Associated Press, http://abcnews.go.com/Business/wireStory?id=4177673, January 23, 2008.

Chapter Eight: Solutions

1. John A. E. Pottow, "The Nondischargeability of Student Loans in Personal Bankruptcy Proceedings: The Search for a Theory," *Canadian Business Law Journal* 44 (March 2007): 245–78.

2. Ibid.

3. Ibid.

4. Mark Kantrowitz, "Impact of the Bankruptcy Exception for Private Student Loans on Private Student Loan Availability," www.FinAid.org, August 14, 2007, www.finaid.org/educators/20070814pslFICOdistribution.pdf.

5. Paul Basken, "Congress May Revisit Bankruptcy Protection for Student Borrowers," *Chronicle of Higher Education,* June 11, 2007.

6. "Government Student Loans, Government Debts and Bankruptcy: A Comparative Study," Office of the Superintendent of Bankruptcy, California, February 27, 2007.

7. "Federal Government Relations Strategy Discussion," obtained from the New America Foundation. See "A Questionable Arrangement," Robert Shireman, May 31, 2007, www.newamerica.net/blogs/education_policy/2007/05/questionable_arrangement.

8. James Daw, "RRSPs to Get Protection under New Bankruptcy Law," www.thestar.com/comment/columnists/article/287971, December 22, 2007.

9. Kelly Field, "Senate Bill Would Allow Borrowers to Discharge Private Student Loans through Bankruptcy," *Chronicle of Higher Education,* September 20, 2007.

10. Blue Dog Democrats voting nay on the amendments were Reps. Baca, Bean, Berry, Bishop, Boren, Cardoza, Carney, Chandler, Costa, Davis, Donnelly, Ellsworth, Giffords, Herseth Sandlin, Hill, Holden, Lampson, Mahoney, Marshall, Matheson, Melancon, Moore, Murphy, Peterson, Ross, , Shuler, Space, Taylor, and Wilson.

11. Larry L. Leslie and Gary P. Johnson, "The Market Model and Higher Education," *The Journal of Higher Education* 45, no. 1 (January 1974): 1–20.

12. Fran Spielman and Dave Newbart, "Cut Half of College Courses," *Chicago Sun-Times,* September 20, 2007.

13. The Education Trust, "Telling the Whole Truth (or Not) about High School Graduation," The Education Trust, Washington, D.C. (December 2003): 1.

Chapter Nine: Practical Advice for Borrowers

1. Steve Friess, "Helicopter School Closes, Leaving Students in Lurch," *New York Times,* February 13, 2008.
2. See www.finaid.org/loantradeoffs.phtml#relief.
3. This applies to Stafford (not Perkins or PLUS), and the graduate student limit is $20,500, no more than $8,500 of which can be subsidized. There are additional unsubsidized Stafford loan limits of $4,000 per year for freshmen and sophomores and $5,000 per year for juniors and seniors and for independent students and students whose parents were denied a PLUS loan.
4. Summary information taken from the Neighborhood Economic Development Advocacy Project, www.nedap.org.
5. *Denittis vs. Educational Credit Management Corp.,* 2007 WL 140955, Bankruptcy District Court, Massachusetts, 2007.
6. Interested readers may wish to research a recent case where this was tested, *Taratuska v. TERI.* See Mark Kantrowitz, "Limitations on Exception to Discharge of Private Student Loans," www.finaid.org/questions/bankruptcylimitations.pdf, August 19, 2007.
7. The basis for this statement lies in an e-mail received from Dr. Greg Walton, who was legislative fellow for Hillary Clinton when the original act was introduced: "By the way, you really started the ball rolling in terms of our office working out some of these issues involving student loans, and putting together a student borrower bill of rights. So thank you for that. Hopefully we can push this issue and make some change."

Appendix

1. Information on stock that was set aside was compiled from SEC form S-8 filings by the Sallie Mae Corporation.
2. Salary information compiled from EdFund IRS form 990 filings.

Index